to the
Great
Secret

The Key to the Great Secret

Rennes le Chateau,
The Holy Grail
and
The Spear of
Human Destiny

T. FINDLEY

Matador
9 Priory Business Park
Kibworth Beauchamp
Leicestershire LE8 0RX, UK
Tel: (+44) 116 279 2299
Fax: (+44) 116 279 2277
Email: books@troubador.co.uk
Web: www.troubador.co.uk/matador

ISBN 978 1780885 377

British Library Cataloguing in Publication Data.
A catalogue record for this book is available from the British Library.

Typeset in 11pt Aldine401 BT Roman by Troubador Publishing Ltd, Leicester, UK

Matador is an imprint of Troubador Publishing Ltd

Contents

Figures	vii
Prologue	ix
The Challenge to Us All	x
Introduction	xi
Chapter 1. The Mystery of Rennes Le Chateau	
– Hoax or No Hoax?	1
Chapter 2. The Paintings by Poussin and Teniers	13
The Shepherds of Arcadia II by Nicolas Poussin	13
The Pentacle in Poussin's painting.	15
1st Reflection	17
2nd Reflection	17
3rd Reflection	17
The D.M. Code and Solution	23
St Anthony and St Paul in the desert by David Teniers	27
The Pentacle in Teniers' Painting	27
The Pentacle in the Landscape	30
The Inscriptions on the Stones	33
Stone no. 1. Upright Tombstone of	
Marie de Negre d'Ables.	34
Stone no. 2. Horizontal Tombstone of	
Marie de Negre d'Ables.	36
Stone no. 3. The Coumesourde Stone.	37
1st Translation	40
2nd Translation	41
Final Translation	41
The Rose-Line	42
Parchment Three	42
Chapter 3. The Meaning of Poussin and	
Teniers' Paintings	49

Definitions   53
The Basic Meditation Technique or Prayer   54
Stage 1 : The Death of the Ego – Black   57
Stage 2 : Purification – White   61
Stage 3 : The Holy Grail – Red   64
Chapter 4. The Implications of the Meaning in
Poussin and Teniers' Paintings   76
Implications for Religion   79
Implications for Psychology, Psychotherapy
and Mental Health   96
Political and Social Implications   108
Implications for Education   118
The Final Implication   127
Chapter 5. Discussion and Conclusion   130

Epilogue   167
Acknowledgements   168
Appendix 1 The Nicene Creed   170
References   171
Bibliography   173

Figures

1.1 *The Shepherds of Arcadia II* by Nicolas Poussin   13
1.2 The angle of 18 degrees between the two staffs.   16
1.3 The Shepherdess' gaze to the heel and extension
    of construction line   19
1.4 The location of the centre of the pentagon   19
1.5 The completed pentagon   20
1.6 The pentacle in the painting   20
1.7 The first reflection   21
1.8 The second reflection   21
1.9 The third reflection   22
1.10 The final complete model   22
2.1 The D.M. code.   23
2.2 Three Vs and an A   24
2.3 Two blocks of four symbols   25
2.4 The eight symbols in their symbolic positions   26
2.5 The D.M. code solution   26
3.1 Henry Lincoln's pentacle in the landscape,
    the three reflections and points A and B   35
3.2 The pentacle in the landscape with
    Poussin's painting superimposed   36
4.1 Stone no. 1. The upright tombstone of Marie
    de Negre d'Ables   38
4.2 Stone no. 2. The horizontal tombstone of Marie
    de Negre d'Ables   38
4.3 Ernest Cros' reproduction of the Coumesourde stone   39
4.4 Gerard de Sede's reproduction of the Coumesourde stone   39
4.5 The M-line cutting the short line in the Coumesourde
    stone and in the landscape   40
5.1 Parchment three with crosses connected spelling out SION   44

5.2 The motif reveals an irregular triangle   44
5.3 Henry Lincoln's irregular pentacle in parchment three   45
5.4 The Rose-Line in the parchment   47
5.5 The Rose-Line with the lines of reflection from
       Montsegur and Puilaurens   47
5.6 The tip of the spear that symbolically pierces Jesus' side   48
6.1 The Chakra System   56
6.2 The Basic Meditation Technique   56
6.3 The arrow that killed Achilles   60
6.4 San greal—Holy Grail. Sang real—Royal Blood   66
6.5 The Holy Grail   69
6.6 The Holy Grail hidden in *The Shepherds of Arcadia II*   70
6.7 The Holy Grail hidden in the landscape   71
6.8 Soul   71
6.9 Spirit   71
6.10 The Star of David   72

Prologue

A common secretive little bird spends its whole day quietly going about its business, seeing but unseen, hearing but unheard, foraging through the undergrowth, picking up bits here and pieces there, scraps and morsels as it needs for sustenance. This humble little bird should not have lived, one moment feeling safe and secure and the next plunged into despair. Nobody knows how that little bird survived those first few days and weeks, and nobody cares, but it did survive and she remembered.

The Challenge to Us All

You are offered the key to a secret door behind which lies the promise of the greatest treasure in the world, but in order to use this key you will have to give away all your possessions, lose your best friend and reject everything you ever believed to be true. Without knowing if this offer is true or false and with only your heart to guide you, would you open the door?

Introduction

An ancient wisdom has been lost to humanity in the mists of time, discarded, rejected, unwanted, disowned, like something cast out, untouchable, waiting patiently to be redeemed. Today this ancient knowledge is known to only a few individuals who keep it a closely guarded secret. This secret knowledge lies at the heart of all world religions and has important implications for the future of humanity. The secret wisdom has been handed down to succeeding generations from the very earliest civilisations from pre-history through the Egyptians to the Greeks and ending up in a little town called Jerusalem 2000 years ago. It is about knowledge of something considered so important by our ancestors that they recorded it permanently in the stars we know today as the Zodiac. These wise men and women also recorded the secret in some of the oldest written texts and orally in myths and legends, so that it would always be accessible to humankind.

The people who wanted to pass down this special message to us have existed in many guises throughout history, but generally have one thing in common: they are all Gnostic in their belief. The most defining feature of all Gnostics is the knowledge that it is possible to have a direct experience of God. Gnostics do not just believe in God, they claim to know God. When Carl Jung was asked if he believed in God, his answer, which puzzled many was, "I don't believe: I know." It was Gnostics who wrote the gospels and it was one group of Gnostics who helped to establish the early Christian Church. It is inconceivable that Gnostics would not have wanted to convey their special knowledge of God to us in their writing, and of course that is exactly what they did and it is that message encoded in the Bible and the gospels based on the ancient wisdom that eventually became the Great Secret.

These became dangerous ideas and over the centuries that followed the death of Jesus this Gnostic message was eventually deemed to be blasphemy by the established Christian Church. At the first council of Nicaea in AD 325 Constantine, the Roman Emperor, decreed what should and should not be included in the Bible and consequently what should and should not be taught to Christians. Many gospels were excluded from the final version of the Bible at this time. Anyone who preached anything other than the official line after this date was in danger of being branded a heretic.

Gnostics were at odds with the now Orthodox Christian Church on two counts. Firstly, Gnostics claimed to have direct access to God. This stance was always bound to be unacceptable to orthodox bishops, priests and the clergy who believed they and they alone should be the sole authority in the Church. Secondly, Gnostic interpretations of the Bible were considered to be a heresy, a rather odd allegation to make against the people who had actually written the gospels. For Gnostics, Jesus was not the son of God, he was just an ordinary man. Orthodox Christian bishops and priests, lacking the secret knowledge, and thus having only a literal interpretation of the Bible open to them, came to such irrational and illogical conclusions that Jesus was the same essence as God, that God was a trinity, Father, Son and Holy Ghost, Mary was able to physically conceive Jesus whilst remaining a virgin, and that one only had to believe in Jesus Christ to be saved and go to heaven. To a Gnostic, this was "the faith of fools".

A literal or a spiritual understanding of the gospels became the dividing issue between Orthodox Christians and Gnostic Christians. For example, the story of Jesus performing miracles by making the blind see was not meant to be taken literally; we know it's impossible. According to a Gnostic understanding, the real meaning of that story is that Jesus opened people's eyes to the reality of God. Those people were blind in that sense only, as we all are. This interpretation makes much more sense in spiritual terms. Opening people's eyes to the reality of God would have been far more important to a Gnostic than curing the blind and is a more enlightened interpretation of a book that is essentially spiritual. At the first council of Nicaea the doors slammed shut on Gnostics and with them went not only their secret knowledge, but also their spiritual interpretation of the Bible. From this date onward there was to be only one understanding of the Bible and that was to be a literal understanding.

Some Gnostic groups continued to exist often in isolation, like the Cathars who lived in a remote region of the Languedoc, South-West France, but even there they were not safe from an increasingly aggressive and intolerant Catholic Church. In 1208 Pope Innocent III proclaimed a formal crusade against the Cathars which began a sustained period of genocide. In 1244, after a prolonged siege at their last stronghold at Montsegur, the Cathars finally surrendered, but rather than renounce their belief, they chose to be burnt at the stake. Legend has it that just before they surrendered, three Cathars escaped down a sheer cliff face, taking the Cathar treasure with them.

Not too many years after this human tragedy, in 1307, Pope Clement V and King Philip IV of France conspired together to wipe out the Templars in a co-ordinated operation that Al Capone or Adolf Hitler would have been proud of. The Templars were Gnostics and the traditional custodians of the Holy Grail and were reported to possess vast wealth. Much to Philip's dismay, no treasure was ever found.

The Catholic Church may have believed they had finally rid themselves of this Gnostic heresy, but Gnosticism did not die out. To escape persecution Gnostics retreated for safety and went undercover, passing on their secret knowledge to each succeeding generation of Gnostics, like an underground stream. The ancient wisdom had always been a secret known only to Gnostics, but now it became doubly so, a secret within a secret organisation. The Gnostic heresy was now the Greatest Secret in the World. The

Gnostic tradition lives on within present day Hermeticism, Rosicrucianism, Alchemy and, if we are to believe Dan Brown, within the Illuminati.

Present day Gnostics believe we live in a modern dark age, living out our lives in an ignorant slumber, never realising our true potential. We are like houses built on sand with just the thin veneer of society shoring up our personalities, holding back our animal nature, existing as just barely civilised apes.

Gnostics have continued their customary practice of encoding the secret knowledge in great works of literature, in art and in particular, enigmatic mysteries. They communicate with each other in this media by producing ever more creative and highly original ways of presenting the great secret, so that fellow Gnostics will know that someone has understood the secret in great detail and a new member has graduated. Traditionally, both in the written word and orally, the secret knowledge is described in terms of the pursuit of a great treasure or the secret location of the Holy Grail. Examples of this exist in the stories of King Arthur and the Knights of the Round Table, the Oak Island Money Pit and the Mystery of Rennes le Chateau. Often the secret is presented quite blatantly within the storyline and yet it remains invisible to us. One even begins to suspect that all these stories are just hoaxes. Even if one feels intuitively that some work may contain a hidden message, that message is elusive and difficult to grasp, as in the case of Alchemy, where the pursuit of gold is written in such a way as to be incomprehensible gibberish. As with all Gnostic writing, it is only understandable if you already know the secret, that is, if you belong to 'the club', but the secret is very well-guarded and this is a very exclusive club. Nobody ever finds out the secret unless they have been initiated into 'the secret order' and they are then bound by an oath of secrecy.

That is until now. From a simple observation and based on my own experience, I know what the Great Secret is and what the Gnostic Heresy was. The implications of this discovery are potentially enormous, e.g. the end of Religion as we know it and a new social and political landscape, one not based on greed and privilege, but on human dignity and compassion for others contained in the notion of Equality, Fraternity and Freedom.

There are two great works of art, one hanging on public display, in which the secret can be revealed in graphic detail. For the first time in public history it is now possible to see the secret explicitly, so there can be no mistaking its existence. What its existence means is open to public debate, but what follows in this book is what it means to me, and if my analysis is right, what I hope it will mean for the future of humanity. It has been said that the secret in one of the paintings would not be found for hundreds of years and the fact that it has been presented in such tangible detail indicates that Gnostics intended it to be discovered eventually. Perhaps when that happened Gnostics would know that humanity was ready for the next step in its evolutionary development, and they would feel free to come forward to guide us. We were not ready 2000 years ago, perhaps we are now. Humanity stands at the threshold of a new dawn, a new age of spiritual enlightenment, a spiritual renaissance when humanity can cast off the shackles of our medieval and superstitious understanding of religion, free ourselves from our selfish and egotistical animal natures and become the caring, compassionate spiritual beings that is our destiny.

What was it then that Gnostics knew that the Catholic Church wanted to wipe from the face of the Earth, what the Catholic Church could not understand and because of that did not want you to know? The truth is often difficult to digest, in this case even more so because this truth will unsettle you, this truth will challenge everything you believe to be true about human nature and the world in which we live, you may find this truth disturbing, but this truth will set you free. This truth brings with it the possibility of a better world based on solid spiritual foundations and humanitarian principles, with the hope for a New Jerusalem.

This book will provide you with the key to understanding the

Great Secret. This key will open your eyes, lifts the veil that surrounds us. In biblical terms it enables the blind to see and the deaf to hear. The real truth behind the mystery of Rennes le Chateau and the reality of the Holy Grail will be clear to you. Those obscure parables in the gospels and the Bible itself will begin to make perfect sense. This is the key to unlock the door to a great treasure; that treasure lies dormant within you, it is your natural inheritance.

What follows is based on my own experience so there are few references. I can only refer you to what exists in your own heart; your heart will know the truth when it sees and hears it. You will need to look closely there, because there you will find yourself, and when you do that you will begin the process of becoming the person you really are, the person you were meant to be. And if you listen carefully to your heart you may hear the sound of one little lost soul crying in the wilderness; this child belongs to each and every one of us, this child of God, pariah of the world, orphan of humanity.

CHAPTER ONE

The Mystery of Rennes Le Chateau – Hoax or No Hoax?

Mysteries, myths and legends fascinate and intrigue us all, with tales of buried treasure and the search for the Holy Grail, as if intuitively we know these stories contain an element of truth that speaks to our very souls, or on the other hand, are they just appealing to our natural greed?

The Oak Island Money Pit is one such case in point. For a small child this story has everything, from pirates to buried treasure, possibly the legendary burial site of the famous Captain Kidd's treasure chest, and an insurmountable and tantalising problem. Oak Island is one of a group of islands just off the coast of Nova Scotia. In 1795 a local man found a small depression on the island with the remains of a block and tackle in the tree above it, as if something had been lowered into the ground. He dug down two feet and hit something hard. With the help of two friends they uncovered a layer of flagstones which covered what appeared to be a filled in shaft. A few years later in 1803 a more organised excavation of the shaft took place. Every three metres down a wooden platform was found and then at twenty-eight metres a mysterious stone with strange characters carved into it. This stone seemed to mark a boundary and to act as a warning not to proceed beyond this point because the next day when the excavation team returned to continue the dig they found twenty metres of water in the shaft which could not be bailed out. Many attempts have been made to reach the bottom of the pit, but so far all have failed due to the flood water, and so far no treasure has ever been found.

So, is the Oak Island Money Pit just a hoax, or is someone eventually going to find a real treasure one day? There are several clues that might indicate it is a hoax. Any mention of pirates and the skull and crossbones should raise suspicions. Pirates sail the seas in search of treasure and the skull and crossbones is a Rosicrucian symbol with a spiritual meaning and probably never used by pirates except in children's stories and films; it wasn't practical, it sort of gave the game away, spoilt that element of surprise. The name Kidd is often used as a substitute for lamb as in the 'lamb of God', and the treasure chest has a spiritual meaning all of its own as will be explained later. The oak also has very strong spiritual connotations. Gnostics and Pagans revere the oak as sacred and venerate it for being the embodiment of universal wisdom. For a more detailed exposition of the subtle ways Gnostics present the secret before us in coded form read, *Hermes Unveiled* by Roy Norvill (1986).

I am more interested in how Oak Island got its name. This is said to have derived from the tree that stood over the pit from which a line was dropped to lower something down the shaft. I do not know if the island had a name before that time, but from that date, the name Oak Island stuck. So, what grows on Oak Island that gives it its name? Oaks! Which sounds like? Yep, hoax. This is the way Gnostics quietly go about their business, gently mocking our ignorance, placing a spiritual secret right before our eyes without us suspecting a thing. This is the stock in trade of the Gnostic writer and these are the literary devices they use to encode the secret within the text, the pun, the sounds-like, the dropping of the letter H, the cryptic clue, the metaphor, the acronym, the analogy, the parable, the anagram, the same word with two meanings one literal, the other spiritual.

The Templars who escaped King Philip fled north to an old fortress at Gisors in northern France taking their treasure with them and from there, some speculate, to England and Scotland and some even say to Nova Scotia. In 1946 a caretaker at Gisors claimed to have found an underground chapel beneath the fortress. He claimed it was an elaborate vault crammed with vast riches including nineteen sarcophagi and thirty boxes full of precious metals. On investigation, all the local town committee found was an unstable hole in the ground, which was quickly filled in for safety. It is claimed that just before it was filled in, a stone dropped down the hole produced an echo, suggesting a large chamber. In 1960 the French Culture Minister ordered a full scale excavation by leading archaeologists. When they failed to find anything the army was called in, but after several months of digging no treasure was ever found.

One of the best examples of the secret being presented blatantly in literature is *The Gold Bug* by Edgar Allan Poe (1845) in which in order to find the treasure, it is necessary to drop a line down through the eye of a skull to pinpoint the exact spot where the gold is buried. The pits at Oak Island and Gisors may or may not be hoaxes, but I believe a theme is emerging here. A mystery, a hidden treasure, a pit or hole in the ground down which a line or stone is dropped in order to reach the treasure, a connection with the Templars, but no treasure ever being found.

In the 11th century Chrétien de Troyes wrote a novel about Perceval and King Arthur's search for the Holy Grail. This was the very first time the Holy Grail was mentioned in literature and, according to experts, appears to have originated entirely from de Troyes' own imagination. So the Holy Grail and all attempts to find it must be a hoax then, surely? But why would anyone go to such elaborate lengths just to fool people? And Oak Island, is that a hoax, and Gisors, just a hoax? The answer is yes *and* no. I want to introduce you to a concept where something can be false and true at the same time, a hoax and not a hoax simultaneously. This paradox involves two opposing concepts, a literal and a spiritual meaning. Oak Island, Gisors, the Holy Grail, are all untrue and therefore, hoaxes in a physical and literal sense, but perfectly true, and therefore, not hoaxes in a spiritual sense. Welcome to the world of the Gnostic story writer, where nothing is ever quite what it seems and often the exact opposite of what you would think.

The mystery of Rennes le Chateau is the Gnostic storyline par excellence, a perfect site in which to base the Great Secret, in a small village on top of a remote hill overlooking the Languedoc just thirty kilometres from Montsegur. This is Cathar country, this is Templar country and this is Grail country. Even the name Rennes is heavy with spiritual meaning as Roy Norvill (1986, p 21) points out; the French word for spider is *araignée*, which sounds almost phonetically identical in the local dialect to *à Rennes* meaning at or around Rennes. The spider is a powerful spiritual symbol in Gnostic terms. Any creature that sheds its skin or outer layer in order to grow to a larger size is holy to a Gnostic because that act symbolises a spiritual process. The snake is revered for its wisdom not only because it sheds its skin, but also because it is closer to nature than any other creature because it glides across the ground. The crab and the scorpion both shed their external skeletons in order to grow and were revered so highly that both were included in the Zodiac. But the greatest symbol of the spiritual process is the spider. Not only does the spider shed its skin, but it also has one other special feature that makes it pre-eminent. It flies on a gossamer thread, sometimes described as symbolic of astral travel, but more accurately an example of how the spider is connected to its web, as the spirit is to the soul: inseparable. Rennes le Chateau is the house of the spider, symbolically the home of the spirit and the soul, the Temple of the soul, symbolically the human spiritual body.

The mystery of Rennes le Chateau begins in 1885 when François Bérenger Saunière is appointed to be the new parish priest at the church of Sainte-Madeleine. The story goes that a few years after his appointment in 1891, whilst carrying out restoration work on the altar, he found four parchments inside three sealed wooden cylinders hidden inside a hollow column supporting the altar. Whatever was written on the parchments was significant enough for the Bishop of Carcassonne to pay for Saunière to travel to Paris to have the documents officially authenticated by the ecclesiastical authorities. Whilst in Paris, it is said, Saunière spent long periods in the Louvre where he purchased reproductions of three paintings.

Whatever knowledge Saunière discovered in the parchments it seems to have had a dramatic effect on his status both socially and financially. Saunière's stock rose, he began to mix with famous people, Emma Calve and Claude Debussy, the most famous people of their day, he became a celebrity amongst celebrities.

On his return from Paris, further excavations were carried out inside the church and according to one of the workers something important was found buried in front of the altar. In the cemetery he erased the engraving on a prominent memorial gravestone as if destroying evidence. Saunière travelled widely over the next two years, opening bank accounts in several main cities in France. Then in 1896 Saunière suddenly started to spend money on a vast scale. Some of this money was spent for the benefit of the villagers. A modern road was built leading up to the village and facilities for running water were provided. He spent large sums on renovating the church often incorporating bizarre and controversial pagan symbolism. He built a tower, the Tour Magdala, on the edge of the hilltop and a lavish country house, the Villa Bethania. Saunière held sumptuous banquets for the villagers, appearing to live the life of a feudal baron. He held court to influential people, most notably Archduke Johann von Hapsburg, cousin of Franz Joseph, Emperor of Austria. By the end of his life Saunière had spent the equivalent in today's money of several millions of pounds. Whatever Saunière found in the parchments it seems to have led him to a treasure that made him a very wealthy and popular man.

After Saunière's death in 1917, interest in Rennes le Chateau waned. People genuinely believed that Saunière had indeed stumbled upon a treasure, but that he had spent it all and there was now nothing left to find. And there it would have remained, just a curiosity from the past and an unexplained rise in the fortunes of a penniless priest. The story goes cold for a number of years and may have been forgotten but for the publication of a book in 1967, *L'Or de Rennes* and in paperback as *Le Trésor Maudit* by Gerard de Sede. It was whilst en route for a summer holiday in France that Henry

Lincoln picked up a copy of this book and found the basis for his Chronicle trilogy on television and also the book *The Holy Blood and the Holy Grail* (1982) in collaboration with Michael Baigent and Richard Leigh.

With the publication of these books, copies of the parchments, supposedly discovered by Saunière, came into the public domain for the first time, for our perusal and to be scrutinised by experts. Of the four parchments, two were apparently genealogies of the Merovingian dynasty and have only recently been published. The third parchment is a story of Jesus and his disciples walking in cornfields on the Sabbath, written in Latin. Certain letters in the text stand out as being slightly out of line with the rest of the text. These letters in isolation spell out a simple message in French:

"A Dagobert II roi et à Sion est ce trésor et il est la mort." The best translation into English is: "To Dagobert II King and at Sion this treasure lies there dormant" (Andrews and Schellenberger, 1996, p 23).

The main body of the text of parchment four describes Jesus' visit to the house of Lazarus. At first sight the parchment is just a meaningless jumble of letters with no spacing between words. A Latin scholar would be able to detect a text was there but concealed by the addition of superfluous letters. Gerard de Sede was able to break the code after a complicated analysis of the additional letters, the final stage being to lay the letters out on two chess boards and then, choosing the right starting point, follow the only sequence of knight's moves that would cover both boards, touching each square only once. The English translation reads:

SHEPHERDESS NO TEMPTATION FOR POUSSIN
TENIERS HOLD THE KEY PAX DCLXXXI BY THE
CROSS AND THIS HORSE OF GOD I REACH THIS
DAEMON GUARDIAN AT MIDDAY BLUE APPLES

So far nobody has been able to provide a satisfactory interpretation of this text. The mention of Poussin and Teniers is encouraging and the obvious suggestion is that it was these artists' paintings that Saunière obtained copies of, but which ones from a whole range of possibilities?

Once again de Sede provides the solution. In *L'Or de Rennes* he suggests the three relevant paintings are *Les Bergers d'Arcadie* by Nicolas Poussin; *St Anthony the Hermit* by David Teniers and a portrait of Pope Celestine V, artist unknown. In a later interview with Henry Lincoln, de Sede had revised his opinion on the Teniers painting, now insisting it was *The Temptation of St Anthony* by David Teniers the Younger that was relevant. However, as Andrews and Schellenberger (1996, p 120) point out, *St Anthony and St Paul in the desert* is the only painting by Teniers to show St Anthony not being tempted. After finally tracing the lost painting, it became clear to them, from the overt geometrical alignments, that this was indeed Teniers' painting referred to in parchment four.

So the impression is that Saunière located the paintings with the help of the fourth parchment and purchased a copy of each from the Louvre. But there are major problems with this explanation as several previous investigators have pointed out. Firstly, only one of these three paintings has ever been exhibited in the Louvre, so copies of the other two would not have been available to purchase there. Secondly, how could Saunière have managed to crack the seemingly impossible cipher code in the fourth parchment and if he did, how would he have known which paintings were important, which leads to, thirdly, the confusion over which three paintings Saunière obtained copies of, because de Sede no longer seems certain. In any case, how does anyone know Saunière bought copies of any paintings at the Louvre? Why would anyone have been interested at that time? This fact only becomes interesting to us in retrospect. Nobody would have been the slightest bit interested back then what he bought, so who recorded this event? Did Saunière or anyone else record it in a diary? If so, then this has never come to light, because if it had we would know exactly which three paintings he purchased. So how could de Sede have possibly known and in which case Saunière may never have purchased any paintings at all and this was planted evidence to create intrigue. If Saunière purchased a copy of any painting at all, it was most likely to have been *The Shepherds of Arcadia II* by Nicolas Poussin, which was on display at the Louvre at the time he visited Paris. This painting was already famous in its own right for being reputed to contain a secret. Painted between 1638 and 1640, Poussin thought so highly of it that he had a relief of it mounted over his tomb. It was regarding this painting that a letter was written to Nicholas Fouquet, Finance Minister to King Louis XIV of France, by his brother Abbé Louis Fouquet, after having spoken with Poussin. The letter reads: "He and I discussed certain things, which I shall with ease, be able to explain to you in detail, things which will give you, through monsieur Poussin, advantages which even kings would have great pains to draw from him, and which, according to him, it is possible that nobody else will ever discover in the centuries to come. And what is more, these are things so difficult to discover that nothing now on this earth can prove of better fortune nor be their equal." (Lepinois, 1656) Shortly after this, King Louis obtained the original painting and kept it at his private apartments at Versailles. If any painting contains a secret then this one is a highly likely candidate. Finally, there is also the problem of the letter W. As it has been stated by several previous investigators, the only way of solving the cipher in parchment four was by working on the assumption of a twenty-six letter alphabet, but in Saunière's day there were only twenty-five letters in the French alphabet. The W was not added until after the 19th century. This is very convincing evidence that parchment four is a modern day forgery.

The trail keeps leading back to de Sede who seems to be the focal point for each new development in the saga. He re-introduced the Rennes mystery to the world. He showed how to work out the cipher in parchment four, a process that required some pre-knowledge of the code. He seemed to know which paintings

Saunière was supposed to have purchased from the Louvre. Where was he getting his information from? De Sede is a member of a secret organisation called the Priory of Sion. The Priory of Sion claims to have had the Holy Grail in its possession for over a thousand years, keeping it safe in a secret location. It also claims to have been founded in the 11th century with links to the Templars and has had many illustrious people in the past as Grandmasters, e.g. Leonardo Da Vinci, Robert Boyle and Isaac Newton.

In a recent television programme, *The Real Da Vinci Code* (Channel 4, 2005), Tony Robinson reveals the Priory of Sion to be an entirely bogus organisation set up to provide some credibility to the current Grandmaster, Pierre Plantard's claim to be the rightful King of France in waiting, a direct descendent of Dagobert II. The programme also revealed that French journalist, Jean-Luc Chaumeil, investigated the Priory of Sion in the 1970s and came to the conclusion that it was all one big hoax. He found that all the documents he looked at led back to three people, Gerard de Sede, Philip de Cherrisey and Pierre Plantard. Chaumeil found that they had created the parchments to give some credibility to the mystery of Rennes le Chateau. Proof of this was provided by showing the original parchments, with an admission of forgery written on them in de Cherrisey's own handwriting. De Cherrisey later confessed to Chaumeil how the whole thing was done. In a later book, de Sede confessed that the whole thing was a hoax and had all been the figment of Plantard's imagination. Plantard himself is also on record, admitting that de Cherrisey invented the code and the cipher.

So is that it then, case solved? The whole mystery of Rennes le Chateau revealed as one big hoax? Tony Robinson came to that conclusion, but there is still the mystery of how Saunière managed to accumulate such vast wealth. Tony Robinson suggests that Saunière made his money by selling masses to whoever would buy and showed Church records which seemed to prove this. From the evidence it seems Saunière was selling masses on a vast scale which was illegal in the Church's eyes and may have accounted for his newfound wealth, but why would he then go on to record his criminality in the Church records for all to see? Saunière's behaviour is that of someone who is immune from prosecution by virtue of some knowledge they hold. There can be no doubt Saunière was making a lot of money from those illegal masses, but there were also other generous donations from wealthy nobles; could it be that Saunière was being paid to reveal the special knowledge that he had gleaned from the original documents as well? One thing can be sure and that is that Saunière was now in the business of making lots of money.

And there we could so easily leave it as obviously just a hoax, but there is still a mystery to solve, but the mystery is now, why would anyone go to such enormous lengths just to fool people, what would be the point, haven't they got anything better to do with their lives? There is still this mystery to solve and with hindsight we can now piece together the probable sequence of events that took place at Rennes le Chateau in 1891. It is probable that Saunière did find some documents, these were not the same documents as parchments three and four that later proved to be forgeries. The documents that Saunière found were not in code, they were quite explicit in their meaning, and this meaning had massive implications for the Catholic Church. He did take these documents to Paris for advice from his seniors about what to do with them, there is evidence he was in Paris at this time. He may never have visited the Louvre even though whilst in Paris it would have seemed the natural thing to do, but I do not think the paintings were important to Saunière except as curiosities. He did not need the paintings, he already had all the information he needed from the documents. That the paintings may also contain the secret is coincidental. I believe the information Saunière discovered was so disturbing to the Catholic Church authorities that they have either kept the original documents locked safely away or they were destroyed, possibly by Saunière himself to stop them from getting into the wrong hands; we know he destroyed the engraving on the gravestone which also seemed to contain the secret knowledge. Perhaps Saunière did not like the implications of the information he had discovered, perhaps the information undermined everything he had ever believed to be true, even undermining the Catholic Church itself. Saunière was then either paid to keep quiet by the Church, sold the secret to wealthy noblemen and women or, as Tony Robinson shows, sold masses illegally, or perhaps even all three.

And there the secret would have remained, locked away, forgotten just as the Church wanted, until the 1960s, when someone, or some organisation, perhaps acting behind the Priory of Sion, decided it was time for the secret mystery to re-appear. This organisation seemed to have knowledge that the secret was contained in certain paintings and by associating those paintings with Rennes le Chateau they could resurrect the mystery. I would like to know how the three men, de Sede, de Cherrisey and Plantard met? Who instigated it? Had they always been friends or associates or did they come together just for this one task and then disband? De Sede is on record as saying that it was all Plantard's idea. Was Plantard the prime mover in all of these events? I have to say, that if Plantard is fraudulent, then he is a very honest sort of fraudster. First he tells us there is no treasure, at least no physical treasure, and then he lets us know that the cipher is a fabrication. Plantard is either a very foolish fraudster or else he is very confident in what he knows, and very focussed on the objective he wants to achieve. I believe he knew the secret.

In the end, it does not matter whether Plantard was a fraud or not; it does not matter that the parchments were forgeries; it does not matter how Saunière made his money; it does not even matter if the Priory of Sion is bogus. What matters is that someone wanted us to look at the paintings by Poussin and Teniers. If there is something important in these paintings, then everything else has been a means to this end. If there is something significant in them, then this is no hoax and everything else that has led us this far becomes irrelevant. And of course there is something in the paintings or else I would not be writing this book. There is something in the paintings that has enormous implications for humanity. What the mystery of Rennes le Chateau conceals is not a vast treasure of precious metals and gems; it is not a Holy Bloodline; it is not Jesus' bones buried in the side of a hill. It is something much more important than that.

Chapter 2

The Paintings By Poussin And Teniers

The Shepherds of Arcadia II by Nicolas Poussin

Fig. 1.1. The Shepherds of Arcadia II by Nicolas Poussin

Take a while to look at Fig. 1.1, *The Shepherds of Arcadia II* by Nicolas Poussin, and if possible, get a larger print to appreciate it fully. This painting is the greatest painting in the history of art, and I can say that with great confidence, even though I am not an art expert, and not because of any technical merit by the artist, or any aesthetic quality it may possess, but because of what it contains. This painting contains the Greatest Secret in the World and as a criteria for assessing a painting's stature, that surely has to rank it in a different league.

As you allow your eyes to roam around the painting they will be drawn to certain prominent features. The two central figures seem to be earnestly trying to locate something by pointing with their fingers, and one looks up as if seeking approval or further guidance. The two standing figures are much more relaxed and confident, reflecting their knowledge of the secret. The standing shepherd and shepherdess are both adepts and are in the process of introducing two initiates into the secret knowledge. The two initiates are trying to understand, but they keep 'missing the point'.

You might also notice the source of the light hidden behind the mountains. Anyone who has been to this spot in South-West France will know that this view faces west, so this painting shows the evening sunset. They will also know that the background immediately behind the subjects is nothing like that depicted in the painting. In reality, the hills are much closer, dominating the landscape, so very little sky would be visible. Yet to the right of the trees, behind the shepherdess, the outline of the hills is exactly the same as from this viewpoint in real life, and that tiny little hillock in the far distance is Rennes le Chateau. Other features in the painting begin to demand our attention, for instance, the two long staffs form an interesting angle between them, which suggests the basis of a pentagon. Henry Lincoln seems to have had some pre-information about the possibility of there being a pentagon in the painting. He brought in Professor Cornford, an expert in the use of geometry in art, to analyse the painting, and he did indeed find a pentagon. The pentagon that Professor Cornford found, had its centre located in the head of the shepherdess, and was so large that some of it existed outside of the painting. Why was Lincoln's investigation so sensitised to the possibility of the painting containing a pentagon? How did this expectation arise? Did de Sede tip Lincoln off again?

That there is a pentagon in the painting, albeit a completely different pentagon to the one that Cornford found, indicates that someone already knew of its existence, and wanted us to find it. However, once the head-centred pentagon mind-set had been established, it became very difficult to see beyond that. Someone did once notice that the two staffs formed the basis for a pentagon, but only to reject it, as yet another example of how one can find a pentagon almost anywhere in the painting, if one tries hard enough. They did not realise how close they had come to the secret.

The Pentacle in Poussin's Painting

From a large print of the original painting, the angle formed between the two long staffs measures 18 degrees, which is exactly what is needed to construct a pentagon, with the staff on the right forming the centre line of the pentagon, and the staff on the left forming one face of the five sides (Fig. 1.2). However, the staffs are quite thick, so to construct the pentagon accurately, one has to decide very early on which side of the left staff to choose. From a large print of the original painting, if one looks carefully, one can see a thin construction line at the left edge of the staff, below the shepherd's hand (Andrews and Schellenberger, 1996) and this seems a promising line of enquiry to follow.

The next stage in the construction of the pentagon requires some inside knowledge of the secret process, and is perhaps why the pentagon has never been discovered before. The knowledge required to access the pentagon is the simple observation, from my own experience, that eyes and heels are the important key elements. The shepherdess appears to look intently at the point that the two initiates are trying to locate, but in fact she is actually gazing through that point, to the heel of the kneeling initiate (Fig. 1.3). It is no coincidence that the extension of the construction line of the left hand staff, also meets this heel point. The heel point is the first point on the concealed pentagon, and the starting point for revealing the whole construction. From this starting point the construction of the pentagon is pure geometry. Measuring 54 degrees from the edge of the staff at the heel point and drawing a line reveals the centre point of the pentagon where this line crosses the long staff on the right (Fig. 1.4). Drawing a circle from the centre point, whose radius is the heel point, the circle intersects the left staff higher up near the shepherd's hand, and this gives the length of each side of the pentagon. It is now just a question of scribing around the circle with dividers and joining the dots to complete the pentagon (Fig. 1.5). The completed geometrical construction contained in the painting is actually a pentacle (Fig. 1.6).

Fig. 1.2. The angle of 18 degrees between the two staffs

In finding the centre point of the pentacle, another decision had to be made: which side of the staff on the right to choose. In the end I chose the centre line of the staff, for reasons that will be apparent later. There was always going to be some leeway in the final positioning of the pentacle due to the uncertainty caused by the thickness of the staffs. In the end, it does not matter if the pentacle is exactly aligned or not, because the pentacle is only a small part of what is concealed in the painting. There is something else concealed within the pentacle.

This painting, *The Shepherds of Arcadia II*, is all about reflected light, and in particular, three hidden reflections: an actual external reflection from the fading sunlight, and two inner spiritual reflections from the shepherdess and shepherd adepts' eyes; an actual reflection symbolising two spiritual reflections. This is the secret that the three reflections reveal, and which is the key to opening that door to a great treasure.

The first reflection

A line running down from the source of light, which passes through the letter A in Arcadia, and then on to the base of the canvas, reflecting back up at an equal angle through the centre line of the staff, to the centre of the pentacle (Fig. 1.7).

The second reflection

A line running down from the eyes of the shepherd, which passes through the letter A in Arcadia, and then on to the hidden heel of the shepherdess, and base point of the pentacle, is reflected back up from the heel to the centre of the pentacle. The line down to the hidden right heel of the shepherdess also passes through the left heel of the initiate, corresponding to the right heel of the initiate on the opposite side of the pentacle (Fig. 1.8).

The third reflection

A line running down from the eyes of the shepherdess, which passes through the Letter A in Arcadia, and then on to the heel of the kneeling initiate, and base point of the pentacle, is then reflected back up from the heel to the centre of the pentacle (Fig. 1.9).

There is one final minor adjustment to make for the model to be complete. So far, for ease of description and portrayal, I have indicated the adepts' eyes as the starting point to symbolise inner reflection. But it is actually the inner eye, represented by the brow that is a more accurate representation of the spiritual process. The nearer those lines move towards the brows of both adepts, the nearer they move towards the tip of the first letter A in ARCADIA inscribed on the tomb. The final completed model, therefore, shows the three lines of reflection and the tip of the letter A, all passing through exactly the same point, point A, and then, after reflecting, all finishing at exactly the same point, point B.

The pentacle is a Gnostic symbol for the human spiritual body. The secret points A and B are physical locations in the human body that correspond with points in the spiritual body; point A is the gateway to our own spiritual natures and the starting point for the development of our true potential. The treasure that this key unlocks is your true self, that child of God. Fig. 1.10 shows the final completed model.

From the completed model it is now possible to see several alignments which would have formed the framework for Poussin's painting. As well as the left staff being in line with the initiate's heel, limbs seem to follow important lines in the model. The left arm of the left adept, the right leg of the left initiate, the left leg of the right initiate with a line from his heel to the centre of the pentacle. The pentacle cross-member cuts through the right initiate's brow and is in line with the edge of the tomb behind the shepherdess. The continuation of the cross-member points directly to Rennes le Chateau on that distant hillock. And what is that in the tree at the tip of the pentacle? Is that a cat's ear? Poussin would have wanted to include a symbol of reflection in his painting, but he knew that if the sun was setting behind the hill, then it was impossible for the

Fig. 1.3. The shepherdess' gaze through to the heel, and the extension of the construction line.

Fig. 1.4. The 54 degree angle to locate the centre of the pentagon.

Fig. 1.5. The completed pentagon.

Fig. 1.6. The pentacle in the painting.

 20

← Base of canvas

Above: Fig. 1.7. *The first reflection.* **Below:** Fig. 1.8. *The second reflection.*

Fig. 1.9. The third reflection.

Fig. 1.10. The final completed model showing point A where the three lines of reflection cross at the tip of the 'A' in Arcadia and point B the centre of the pentacle.

greatest symbol of reflection, the moon, to be behind the tree. So he chose the second best symbol of reflection, the cat. The cat was revered by the Egyptians because its eyes reflected light in the dark, a perfect representation of the secret process. Poussin put a cat in the tree looking straight down the centre line of the staff and pentacle and main reflection in the painting. Poussin had a sense of humour, it is indeed a cat's ear; the ear implies two hidden cat's eyes.

The validity of any model rests on two main requirements, that it can accurately predict something that has not been known before and that it consistently solves problems that have been unsolvable in the past. A prediction my model makes is that there is more of Poussin's painting hidden under the base of the frame on the left hand side of the painting than on the right and the angle this creates is just enough to make the reflection from the setting sun exact. This model has already accurately solved one seemingly impossible puzzle, but it can also solve others. The fact that I know this model works is not important, it is how I came to know, and that grew from my own experience. In a way, my experience validates the model, just as the model validates my experience, in a kind of mutual validation. I could not have discovered the secret in the painting without having had that experience and the secret in the painting confirms my experience as genuine. But there is more evidence that gives validity to the model.

The D.M. Code and Solution

O . U . O . S . V . A . V . V
D .   M.

Fig. 2.1. The D.M. code.

The D.M. Code (Fig. 2.1) is a series of letters inscribed on a monument underneath a mirror image reproduction of the Shepherds of Arcadia in the grounds of Shugborough Hall in

Staffordshire. The inscription has never been satisfactorily deciphered even by the best code-breakers in Britain. If my model can crack this code, then surely, that would validate it and thus the theory on which it is based. The depiction of the Shepherds of Arcadia on the Shepherd's Monument is mysteriously a mirror image of the original painting. This fact has never been satisfactorily explained either, but when one considers that the entire painting is based on reflection, then a mirror image is very appropriate, and indicates that whoever was responsible for creating this monument, understood this underlying principle, and used it in an original way.

For a long time, the letters D and M were difficult to interpret, being separated from the main text. The D and M are actually set apart from the main text because they are not part of the secret code. In ancient Rome, the manes or Di Manes were deities who protected the souls of deceased loved ones. Roman tombstones often included the letters D.M. which stood for 'diis manibus' (for the Manes), an inscription that continued to appear even in later Christian inscriptions. D.M. is a reference to an old Gnostic tradition, and indicates that the monument is dedicated to the spirits of the dead (Wikipedia).

The first thing to realise about the remaining letters is that they are not meant to be read as letters at all, but as symbols for something else. These symbols, when read correctly, give instructions about how to find the secret in the painting. If the symbols are separated down the middle (Fig. 2.2), it can be seen that the four symbols on the right, three Vs and an A may seem familiar

O U O S | V A V V

Fig. 2.2.

with regard to what has previously been discussed. If one had to graphically convey the meaning, 'reflection', with one symbol, it would be the letter V. The letter V is a perfect symbol of reflection. The D.M. code is referring to three reflections and an A hidden in the painting as predicted in the model (Fig. 1.10). But the A is also a symbol of something else, as is the A in Arcadia. When one looks at the letter A one can also see an arrowhead or the tip of a spear. The A in this instance symbolises the tip of a spear. The symbols on the right of the code are suggesting three reflections in the painting, but where are they? The four symbols on the left of the code provide the answer to this, by defining specific locations for those three reflections. Of the four symbols on the left, the Os symbolise both the outer light source from the setting sun and the inner light source from the adepts' brows. The U is a symbol for the heel because it is the perfect outline of a heel when viewed from the rear. The S can be a symbol for the sun, a staff or a snake. But following the logic of the rest of the formulae, and by the process of deduction, there was only one factor missing from the equation, a symbol for the base of the canvas, a baseline. The S signifies a snake in this instance, a symbol of wisdom, but also a symbol for the ground on which it glides, the baseline. All the symbols in the code are exactly the same in a mirror image, except the S, which is still a snake whichever way you look at it.

There is one more important rule to understand about how the code works. The symbols have to be divided into two blocks of four for a specific reason. The two blocks of symbols have to be read in conjunction with each other, so as they are read across the Shepherd's Monument, from left to right, the two blocks of symbols are read simultaneously left to right also (Fig. 2.3).

O U O S
V A V V

Fig. 2.3.

The top block of four symbols can now be placed in their appropriate symbolic positions (Fig. 2.4).

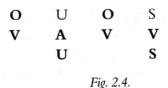

Fig. 2.4.

Now each symbol has been defined and placed in its appropriate symbolic position, it is possible to read the symbols across the Shepherd's Monument, from left to right. If one reads the painting from left to right, the first point arrived at is the shepherdess' brow O^1, and the first reflection V^1 down to the initiate's heel at U^1 (Fig. 2.5). Continuing the scan across the painting, the next point arrived

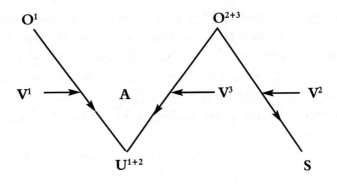

Fig. 2.5. The D.M. code solution.

at is the symbol A, which is the A in Arcadia, and as we have seen, very much associated with the three reflections and included with them for this reason, but plays no active part in the code; nevertheless it, remains the most important symbol in the code. The third point arrived at is the source of light from the setting sun O^2, and the second reflection V^2, down to the base of the canvas S. The final point arrived at is the shepherd's brow O^3 and third reflection V^3 down to the shepherdess' heel U^2. There is an economy in the use of symbols, using only one U for both heels and two Os for three reflections, but that makes the code beautifully concise.

The Vernon family, who commissioned the Shepherd's Monument, may have wanted to leave their initials on the monument in remembrance of themselves, but they were also using those initials to tell us of something much more important than themselves, which seems to be a particular trait of all Gnostics.

St Anthony and St Paul in the Desert By David Teniers the Younger

There is some dispute about which Teniers painting is referred to in the mystery of Rennes le Chateau. Initially, de Sede suggested *St Anthony the Hermit*, but later insisted it was *St Anthony and St Paul in the desert*, that should be looked at. Later research by Baigent, Leigh and Lincoln (1982), pinpointed *St Anthony and St Jerome in the desert*, because that was the only Teniers painting they had ever seen in which St Anthony is not being tempted. There seems to be some confusion over which painting, which Teniers and which title. Perhaps the confusion is caused by the possibility that the Teniers' may have concealed the secret in several of their paintings, especially those depicting St Anthony. In the end, it does not matter which Teniers painting everyone agrees is the correct one, all I know is, the painting *St Anthony and St Paul in the desert* by David Teniers the Younger contains the secret.

The Pentacle in Teniers' Painting

I am not allowed to show you an image of *St Anthony and St Paul in the desert* by David Teniers the Younger because this would infringe the copyright law. I cannot put this image in my book because I have been unable to obtain permission from the owner of the copyright. I have been unable to obtain this permission because nobody appears to know who the copyright owner is. This, when the artist has been dead for over 100 years, the painting has been in the public domain for almost as long and the importance of the knowledge that this legislation restricts. Because of this restriction, you may wish to obtain your own copy of the image and using the following instructions construct your own pentacle in Teniers' painting. Take a while to look at *St Anthony and St Paul in the desert* by David Teniers the Younger, the image is freely available on the internet and is distinguishable from others by the tau on St Anthony's upper right sleeve. This painting is the second greatest painting in the history of art, et cetera. Notice some of the important features. St Paul seems to be trying to teach St Anthony something and gestures to a bird in the sky carrying what appears to be food in its beak. Another bird in the distance may be coming this way, following the first bird, implying a steady supply of food, and that village on the hill, could that possibly be a reference to Rennes le Chateau? Bizarrely there is a skull on the plinth in front of a small crucifix of Jesus Christ, which sits at an odd angle. The staffs or walking sticks make an interesting angle, but not with each other this time. The general line of St Paul's stick points to his left eye, which appears prominent. However, it is known from the Poussin painting that the brow is likely to be the key starting point. St Paul's stick is slightly curved, but the top of it, in his hand, points directly to his brow, and this angle is approximately 70 degrees to the bottom of the painting. The odd angle at which the crucifix leans, is approximately 2 degrees to the vertical. Therefore, the angle between the line of the top of the stick and the line of the crucifix is 18 degrees. The other stick resting on the plinth is generally pointing to the base of the crucifix. Expecting the existence of a hidden pentagon one can make the assumption that the centre line of the crucifix at its base is the centre of that pentagon. An angle of 54 degrees drawn from the line of the stick drawn at the brow confirms this point as the centre of the pentagon. Taking the distance from the centre point to the brow as the radius of the pentagon, a circle can be drawn. Where this radius crosses the line of the stick lower down and the line of the crucifix at the top gives the length of the sides of the pentagon. Scribe round the circle with dividers and join the dots to complete the pentagon and reveal the hidden pentacle.

This painting is also about reflection, but in this case it is not light that is being reflected. What is being reflected in this painting is the notion of what is being carried in the bird's beak. It looks like bread, but this is no ordinary bread, as the Welsh would sing, this is 'bread of heaven', manna from heaven, spiritual nourishment from God.

It is now possible to observe several important alignments in the painting, too many to be pure chance. There are three main reflections from the nearest bird. The first reflection travels down from its beak through the eye of the skull to the base point of the pentacle and then back up the line of St Paul's stick to his brow. The second reflection travels down from its beak through the centre point of the pentacle, to the base of the painting and back up along the line of St Paul's stick to his brow. The third reflection travels down from its beak to the base of the painting and back up through the eye of the skull. The eye of the skull is a key point and reminiscent of the story by Edgar Alan Poe, where a line had to be dropped down through the eye of a skull to locate the treasure. There is an alignment with St Paul's brow, his thumb and index finger, and the distant bird. The distant bird has a reflected line, running from its beak, which connects it with the base of the painting at the centre line of the pentagon, and St Paul's brow. There is also an alignment that runs from the distant bird, through the centre of the pentacle then through the eye of the skull, to a jar on the left of the painting. This jar is also in alignment with the near bird's beak and St Paul's index finger. Two of the near bird's three reflected lines are equally reflected with reference to the plane of the pentagon, and the distant bird's reflected line is equally reflected to the plane of the painting. The cross-member of the pentacle points to that village on top of the hill, the same as Poussin's pentacle. It is therefore clear from the alignments that there are two key points in the painting, the eye of the skull and the centre of the pentacle corresponding with points A and B in Poussins' painting. And what's that in the rocks that St Paul gestures to, is it a bears' head? It is indeed a bears' head, the Great Bear a symbol for Ursa Major and Arcadia.

The Pentacle in the Landscape

Henry Lincoln appears to have had some expectation of the possibility of there being a pentacle in Poussin's painting. Was this because of his discovery of a pentacle in parchment three or did de Sede tip him off in both respects? The existence of a pentacle in the painting, not the one that Professor Cornford found, demonstrates that someone knew of its existence and wanted us to find it. Even though Professor Cornford's pentacle was wrong in terms of the secret, his pentacle has some credibility in terms of the golden ratio, which Poussin would have used to set out his masterpiece. The centre of his pentacle pinpoints the Shepherdess' brow and allowing for the hidden canvas beneath the frame, that line down to the base of his pentagon would have in fact followed the line of reflection three through the A in Arcadia down to the initiate's heel, but without knowing the secret key this fact was missed. Professor Cornford's addition to the quest for the solution to the mystery was his suggestion to try and find alignments in the map of the area even though this was beyond his expertise. Henry Lincoln duly found a remarkable alignment in the landscape, a triangle of castles, Rennes le Chateau, Blanchefort and Bezu that suggested the basis of a pentacle and just as remarkable the remaining two points of the pentacle coincided with peaks in the area also (Lincoln, 1991). This is a naturally occurring feature of the landscape, but this topographic coincidence of peaks did not go unnoticed by the Templars who eventually built the three castles as part of a much grander and more monumental plan for the area. The Templars liked subtlety, notice how nothing is presented openly, always hidden just beyond our reach; to have built a castle on each peak would have been far too obvious, but the three castle peaks on their own just leaves that element of doubt. Nevertheless, once found, its argument is compelling.

For a long time I considered the lines and alignments in the landscape surrounding Rennes le Chateau to be much of a red herring having already discovered the secret in the paintings. I arrived at the secret of Rennes le Chateau from an entirely different direction to Henry Lincoln, starting from a spiritual understanding and working back towards the physical and topographical features in order to make sense of the mystery, whereas Lincoln and others start from the physical and topographical and reach out to the unknown. So in order to provide some verifiable data to support my discovery I revisited the maps and their intriguing alignments. Henry Lincoln's pentacle in the landscape was of particular interest and it was whilst examining those features that I began to realise that the alignments in the landscape, fixed by the castles they connected, predated Poussin's painting by hundreds of years, in which case it was highly probable that Poussin's painting could be a replica, a record, a representation on canvas of what was already there in the landscape and furthermore, if that was the case then perhaps the three lines of reflection and points A and B are there represented in the landscape also. I was consequently looking tentatively just north of the little village Lavaldieu for point A in my model Fig. 1.10, and something that the Templars may have left to mark this spot, so you can imagine the 'eureka' moment when I found the small pentacle in a field exactly where it was supposed to be. One of the points of the pentacle has been worn away probably by grazing animals so that viewed from above, X literally marks the spot. I would say at this point to all you treasure seekers hoping to find the Templar treasure not to waste your time trying to find a physical treasure at Lavaldieu. Anyone who goes digging for treasure at Lavaldieu is wasting their time, and will never understand the real meaning of this treasure. What you see is all there is, just a pentacle on the ground marking the spot. This spot does indeed mark the Templar treasure, but this is a hidden invisible treasure. Before you start digging, you need to understand that this is a spiritual treasure not a physical treasure, and afterwards, all you will find is a hole in the ground.

Henry Lincoln, David Wood, and Andrews and Schellenberger found many fascinating and intriguing alignments in the landscape around Rennes le Chateau over the years, which has become quite a complex matrix of inter-connected networks, but the complexity of which misses the whole point. Henry Lincoln should return to his basic idea and assess it with an open mind. There is a problem with his original triangle of castles at Rennes le Chateau, Blanchefort and Bezu: the angle at Blanchefort is not exactly 72 degrees. The pentacle that Lincoln found needs only a minor adjustment in order for the alignments I am suggesting to occur, e.g. the line from Blanchefort to the castle at Bezu is almost parallel to the Paris Meridian line, too close not to have been intended. This confirms that Blanchefort is slightly out of line to form a perfect pentacle, but if one forms a perfect pentacle taking Rennes le Chateau and Bezu as the initial fixed points, then all the alignments fall into place and now the sunrise line over Blanchefort and Arques from Rennes le Chateau is also parallel with the opposite side of the pentacle. Looking from this new position at the point of the pentacle near Blanchefort over Roque Negre the line of direction meets the point of the pentacle that touches the Paris Meridian line as *Le Serpent Rouge* tries to inform us. Le Pique is not quite the centre of the pentacle, this point, point B, being located tens of yards further north-west hidden in trees. Henry Lincoln found a mysterious pool at this spot, built of stone to the same dimensions apparently as Poussin's tomb, but sadly nothing remains to be seen of it today due to treasure seekers (Henry Lincoln's website). Tragically this pool, was the physical symbolic representation of the Holy Grail here on earth, the like of which will never be seen again. Interestingly, the small pentacle at Lavaldieu, Le Pique, the centre of Henry Lincoln's pentacle and Rennes le Chateau are all aligned and this is no coincidence (Fig. 3.1). As with the paintings, it does not matter whether the pentacle in the landscape is exactly aligned or not, it is the three reflections and what they indicate that are important.

The three reflections hidden in the landscape which pinpointed point A at Lavaldieu are, firstly, the setting sun behind Mount Cardou on one particular day of the year, aligning with the church at the village Le Bezu, passing just north of Lavaldieu to the Paris Meridian before reflecting back to the centre of the pentacle. Poussin used some artistic licence here by removing the entire mass of mount Cardou and replacing it with a much smaller version which in appearance looks suspiciously like the castle Bezu. The second reflection is quite staggering in its audacity and precision. I was considering something important to the Templars, something that would be highly symbolic for them which they might have used to represent the lines of reflection from the shepherdess and the shepherd's brows. Now what are the chances that a straight line from Montsegur, travelling some thirty kilometres, would pass just north of Lavaldieu to meet the Paris Meridian line exactly where Henry Lincoln's pentacle touches it and then reflect back to the centre of the pentacle, but amazingly it does and this is not pure chance. The third reflection is just as audacious, travelling all the way from the castle at Puilaurens, passing through Lavaldieu on its way to Blanchefort where it reflects back to the centre of the pentacle. The Shepherdess is the symbol for Montsegur and the Shepherd is the symbol for Puilaurens, the adepts who guard the secret in 'God's Valley' from a distance, always vigilant, keeping a watchful eye. But now, entirely in concordance with the features in the landscape, Poussin's painting can be laid out on a map of the area with all its alignments and fit precisely (Fig. 3.2).

The Inscriptions on the Stones

There are three well-known stones associated with the mystery of Rennes le Chateau; two gravestones and an inscribed stone found at Coumesourde. There is some doubt about the authenticity of two of these stones, but there is no doubt that one of them actually existed, being recorded by an independent source. The first two stones are linked to Marie de Negre d'Ables' grave at Rennes le Chateau. The first of these two stones was an upright stone and is the stone that Saunière defaced, but the existence of which was verified by the Aude Society for Scientific Studies prior to its destruction. The second of these stones has been described as a horizontal stone laid on top of the same grave. The doubt regarding its authenticity arises from the fact that the above society did not record its existence on the same day that they recorded stone number one's existence even though it would have been just as important to them (Putnam and Wood, 2003). The third stone is the Dalle of Coumesourde which was supposedly found in 1928 buried under an *oak* tree in a crevice in the rocks at Coumesourde. Any artefact found in this way would always arouse suspicions surrounding its authenticity. However, this raises an important issue of whether an object has to be authentic in order to add to a body of knowledge if its purpose is to enlighten us.

The two unauthenticated stones are still valid evidence in the search for the secret because they reveal the truth and were created by someone who knew the secret. Each stone reveals a different part of the secret and together they form the whole truth.

Stone no. 1 (Fig. 4.1) is the upright tombstone of Marie de Negre d'Ables. At first sight this stone looks crudely carved and yet on further investigation these apparent errors are deliberate. The M in Marie stands alone, the O in the date should not be there, the R in DARLES should be a B, and the first word should be ICI, the first letter missing having been weathered away. These four letters together with the four oddly carved small letters give MORT epee. Now MORT EPEE happens to be the keyword for solving the cipher in parchment four. However, since parchment four was recently proved to be a modern day forgery there must have been

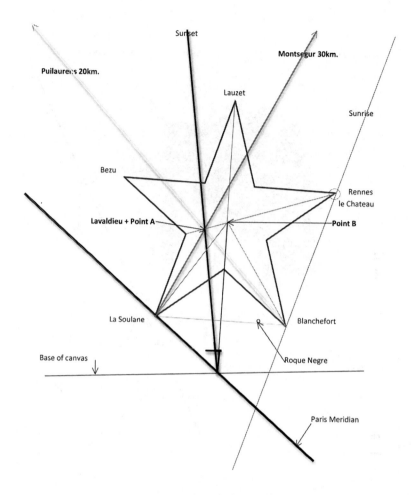

Fig. 3.1. Henry Lincoln's pentacle in the landscape with the three reflections and points A and B.

some other important reason why Saunière destroyed this tombstone. MORT EPEE literally translates as "death by sword", but the sword is also a symbol for air, so this phrase is referring to a death brought about by the function of our breath acting like a pointed blade. The meaning is obscure and one wonders why

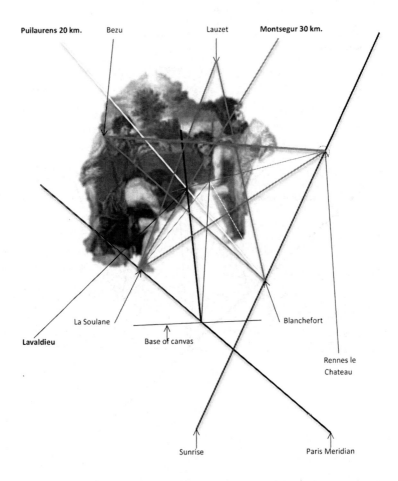

Puilaurens 20 km. Bezu Lauzet Montsegur 30 km.

La Soulane
Lavaldieu
Base of canvas
Blanchefort
Rennes le Chateau
Sunrise
Paris Meridian

Fig. 3.2. Henry Lincoln's pentacle in the landscape with Poussin's painting superimposed.

Saunière still felt the need to destroy the stone? Perhaps he was taking no chances, because that is what it does mean, that is all it can mean in this context, as will later become clear.

Stone no. 2 (Fig. 4.2) is the horizontal tombstone of Marie de

Negre d'Ables and is probably a fabrication by the same people behind whoever forged the parchments. The two vertical rows of Roman letters when translated into Greek become ET IN ARCADIA EGO (Lincoln, 1991). Henry Lincoln gives a good account of the possible meaning of the P S with the loop around it by linking it with PRAE–CUM. PRAE means 'before' and CUM means 'with' so the loop around P S is referring to what comes before the P and before the S which is O and R and OR in French is gold which appears to be linked 'with' the spider in some way (Lincoln, 1991). The four remaining words REDDIS REGIS CELLIS ARCIS literally mean "the return of the king from the cellar of the castle." Lincoln loses faith in his own analysis at this point, but he nearly arrived at the truth. The gold is the treasure that lies there waiting to be found within you. You are the King/Queen waiting to be freed from your own prison in the cellar of your own castle, your own spiritual body, and the spider is symbolic of the process of regeneration, of death and rebirth that is required to achieve that.

Stone no. 3 is the Coumesourde stone and which is probably another fabrication, but which actually accurately reveals the secret in more detail. The Coumesourde stone was found in 1928 by Ernest Cros a part time archaeologist and an old friend of Saunière. None of these three stones exist anymore, but Cros reproduced this copy of the engraving prior to its destruction (Fig. 4.3). The reproduction most often cited is the one by Gerard de Sede (Fig. 4.4), the only difference being in Cros' reproduction of the original, the S and the PS PRAECUM are outside the triangle. Corjan de Raaf and Jean-Pierre d`Aniort (undated) made the simple observation that the engravings on the Coumesourde stone were probably Roman abbreviations, e.g. CAE short for CAESAR. Based on the common method of abbreviation they arrived at two possible translations of the stone's inscriptions depending on which reproduction was being analysed, Cros' or De Sede's.

```
ICT  GIT  NOBLe  M

ARIE  DE  NEGRe

DARLES  DAME

DHAUPOUL  De

BLANCHEFORT

AGEE  DE  SOIX

ANTE  SEpT  ANS

DECEDEE  LE

XVII  JANVIER

MDCOLXXXI

REQUIES  CATIN
```

Fig. 4.1. The engravings on stone no. 1.

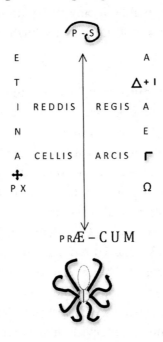

Fig. 4.2. The engravings on stone no. 2.

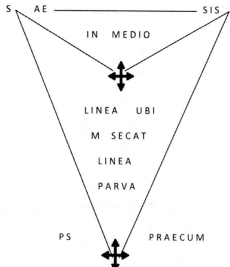

Fig. 4.3. Ernest Cros' reproduction of the Coumesourde stone.

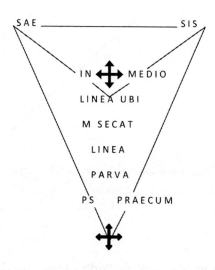

Fig. 4.4. Gerard de Sede's reproduction of Cros' Coumesourde stone.

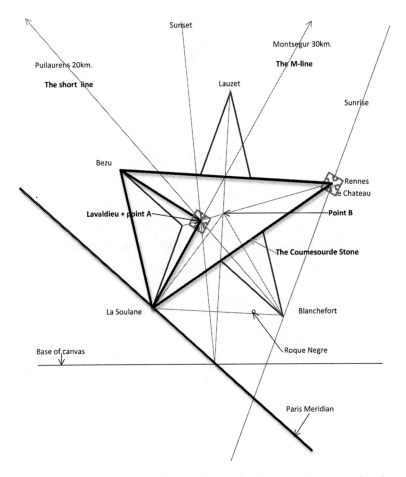

Fig. 4.5. The M-line cutting the short line in the Coumesourde stone and in the landscape.

First translation based on de Sede's reproduction.

In this translation SAE is short for SAECULUM and SIS short for

SISTERE. SAECULUM means 'forever' and SISTERE means to 'last' or 'endure'. Therefore, SAECULUM SISTERE relates to something that will 'survive forever'. PS is short for PIIS , The Holy One. PRAE and CUM are short for PRAETOR CUMPRIMIS or PRAETOR CUMLATUS which means 'first of the leaders' or 'crowned leader'. De Raaf and d`Aniort's conclusion of translation number one is that the Coumesourde stone can lead us to a place where something that can survive forever can be found and has to do with a crowned leader or Holy One.

Second translation based on Cros' reproduction.

This is probably the more accurate reproduction of the two and where the S is separate from AE and exists outside of the triangle as does the PS and PRAECUM all appearing to have been deliberately placed there for a good reason. Outside the triangle is S, PS and PRAECUM and inside are AE IN MEDIO SIS LINEA M UBI SECAT LINEA PARVA. Following the same logic of abbreviations gives SEPULCRUM PATRI SUO PRAEDIS CUM, literally meaning 'In the tomb with the riches of the forefathers where the treasure lies'. AGNUM ELATUS IN MEDIO SIS LINEA M UBI SECAT LINEA PARVA literally meaning 'The lamb brought in the middle for burial where M-line cuts the short line'. De Raaf and d'Aniort's conclusion of translation number two is "that something defined as the lamb was buried with a great treasure and the M-line plays a central role as to where that is" (p 1).

The final translation of De Raaf and d'Aniort's two translations is that both translations are valid and de Sede was well aware of this when he made the modifications to Cros' original reproduction. The Coumesourde stone is telling us that there is a secret place where a great treasure can be found that has survived the ages and will endure for evermore. But this treasure is not a physical treasure, it is a spiritual treasure, the gift of your own true spiritual self. You are the crowned leader, the King/Queen in waiting, and the secret place is where we can find Jesus within ourselves. Jesus is the lamb, the lamb of God who has to be sacrificed within you on your own cross so that you may reach the Kingdom of God and spiritual immortality. And this secret place can be found where the M- line cuts the short line. The M-line is the line from Montsegur, the Shepherdess' gaze, which cuts the short line from Puilaurens, the Shepherd's gaze, at Lavaldieu, point A (Fig. 4.5). The interpretation of all three stones combined is that Jesus, the lamb of God, has to be sacrificed on the cross within you in order for you to be reborn and to be freed from your self-imposed prison/tomb, so that you may live forever in the Kingdom of God, see chapter 3.

The Rose-Line

'The Rose-Line' is the name given to the brass line laid into the floor of the Church of Saint-Sulpice in Paris, to define the exact time of Easter and also known as the red serpent. This line is often confused with the Paris Meridian, but they are not the same, being separated by some one hundred metres at Paris. However, due to the curvature of the earth and like the segment of an orange, by the time these two meridians reach the Languedoc region they are some 1000 metres apart. A Priory of Sion document 'Au Pays de la Reine Blanche' (1967) states that "Rennes les Bains is located precisely on the Zero Meridian, which connects Saint-Sulpice in Paris", and also, "the line of the Zero Meridian, that is to say the red line, in English: 'Roseline'", and Pierre Plantard also referred to the "red line of the meridian, the 'Rose-Line'. . ."(Wikipedia). It would appear that the Rose-Line is extremely important to the Priory of Sion and consequently to the region around Rennes le Chateau.

Parchment No. 3

Parchment three as well as giving a straightforward overt message also contains a more covert message. Henry Lincoln found some unusual alignments in this parchment that appeared to be associated with the mysterious motif in the top left hand corner and some odd crosses contained within the text and when these crosses were joined with a line it spelt out the word SION (Fig. 5.1). This seemed to be a promising lead and when the motif also aligned with these points he knew he was on to something (Fig. 5.2) and further analysis revealed a hidden irregular pentacle (Fig. 5.3). Henry Lincoln seems to be the one who makes all the critical breakthroughs in this mystery, and others that come after him use his discoveries to then go off at a tangent. So was Lincoln being prompted by de Sede to make all these discoveries, but without being given the entire secret? I think he was and which would explain Lincoln's adherence to his original discoveries and why he remains today much closer to the truth than all those who followed him.

The motif in parchment three needs some explaining and only Andrews and Schellenberger have genuinely attempted this. This motif could refer to the M-line or it could refer to a Meridian line, but it can also indicate a point breaking through something, as Henry Lincoln suggests. Andrews and Schellenberger turn Lincoln's irregular triangle into a regular triangle to suit their own ends. However, the pentacle in the parchment does not have to be regular, it is only symbolic of a regular pentacle. A regular pentacle within the parchment would have meant the text was unworkable; that any sort of pentacle is made possible within the text is remarkable in itself. Anyway we have already seen that the pentacle is not the most important part of the secret, the three reflections and points A and B and their alignments are, and the fact that the pentacle could be made irregular is confirmation of this.

Andrews and Schellenberger show that the M over I in the motif is an alignment, confirmed by the M over I at the bottom left hand corner of the parchment which gives a line or plane of alignment. The only other M over I occurs in lines 4 and 5 of the parchment and which becomes clear, is to be parallel with the M over I line in the motif. This line, from lines 4 and 5, is the most important line that the parchment was designed to both hide and reveal, this is the

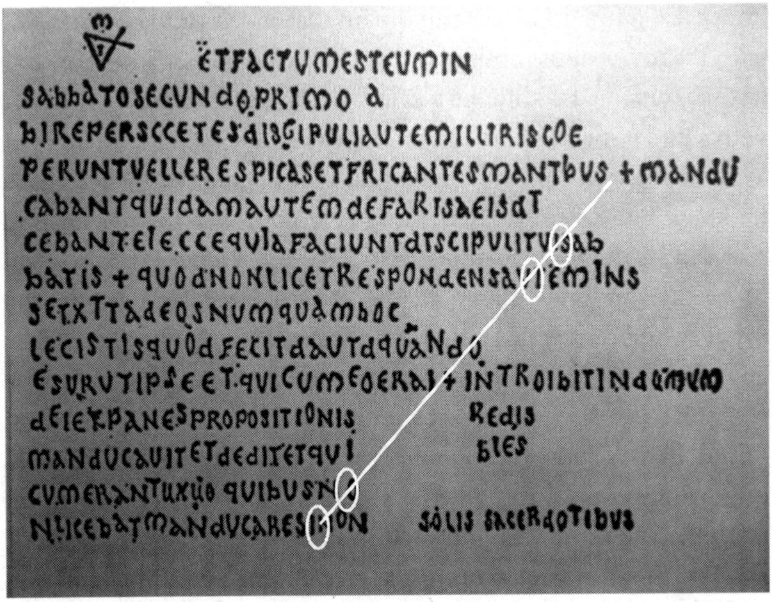

Fig. 5.1. Parchment three with the crosses connected spelling out SION.

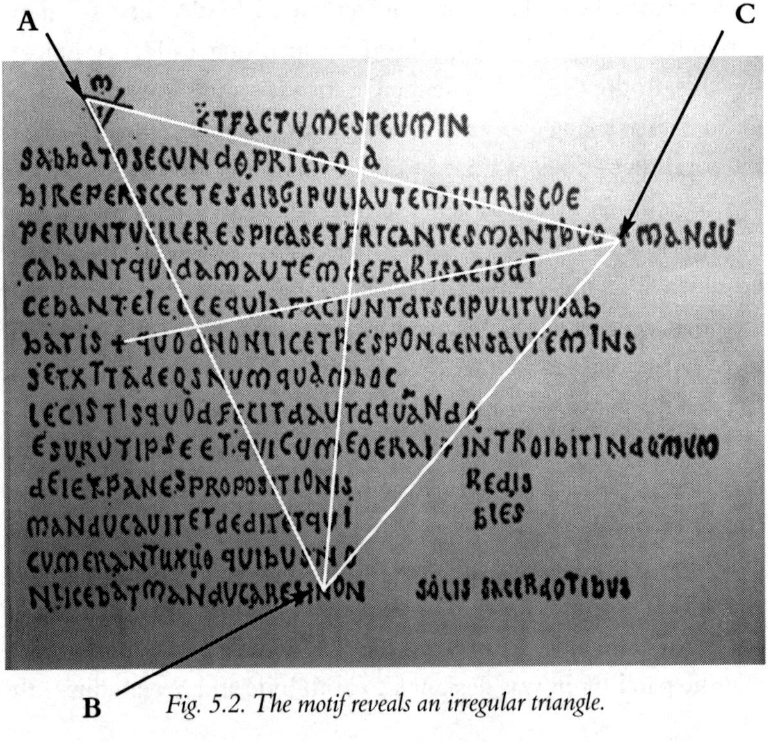

Fig. 5.2. The motif reveals an irregular triangle.

44

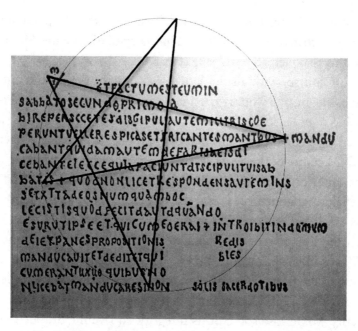

Fig. 5.3. Henry Lincoln's irregular pentacle in parchment three.

Rose-Line in the parchment and which is also parallel with Henry Lincoln's line that bisects points A and C in his original triangle (Fig. 5.4). The symbolic lines of reflection coming from Montsegur and Puilaurens pass through one particular letter in the parchment. If these two lines had passed through any other letter then that lead would have gone cold, but this letter is an M which confirms we are on the right track. Now there is something about the letter M as it is written in the parchment which you may not have noticed. When I was a *kid*, there were two things I used to draw like that, a *bird* flying in the distance and a *spider*. The two lines of reflection pass through the spider/bird, which also happens to be on the centre line of the symbolic pentacle. It can now be seen that whichever way you look at it, where the M-line cuts the short line is point A in my model (Fig. 1.10), a point where a regenerative transformation takes place, symbolised by the spider, and where spiritual food is digested, symbolised by the bird. It can now also be seen that the point of the pentacle that pierces the Rose-Line is symbolic of the Spear of Destiny that pierced Jesus' side (Fig. 5.6).

Of course, with all the letters available in the parchment to choose from, one would expect to be able to spell out any word one wishes in order to confirm one's own particular theory or bias. For instance, I could point out that the two lines after being reflected and the centre of the pentacle in Fig. 5.5 cut through one letter and one letter only and that is the I in line 4, the I in PIC, which is French for mountain peak and could be referring to Le Pique which sits exactly in that position in the landscape. Or I could point out that the line of reflection coming from Puilaurens cuts through PULIAU in line 3 and RESIN in the last line and I am sure that some of the more discerning amongst you will probably be able to find MONTSEGUR somewhere in there. I could, but then my theory would lose some of its integrity, so I won't. Suffice to say when one knows what the secret is, all these things stand out as being obvious, and knowing what I know, I am able to look at the evidence with a kind of hindsight. But now it can be seen that the motif in the top left hand corner of parchment three is not just a plane of alignment that reveals the Rose-Line but, also indicates that there are two important letters in the text , the M and the I, which correspond with points A and B in the landscape and the paintings.

You may find the next few chapters disturbing, unsettling, troubling, worrying; they may turn your world upside down, they will certainly challenge everything you believe to be true. This knowledge may make you angry, confused, inspired, happy, distraught, rejoiceful, contemptuous, amused, sad or hopeful, and I will be pleased for you, because with these emotions, you will become aware of your unconscious and from that can bring about change. The truth is sometimes uncomfortable, but that should not make one shy away from it. I give you the Great Secret, look after it, care for it, nurture it, treat it with kindness, with gentleness and with tenderness, respectfully; it will repay you.

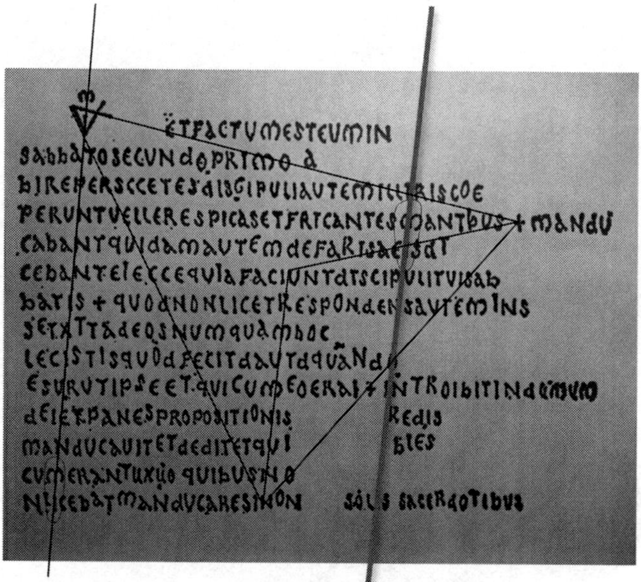

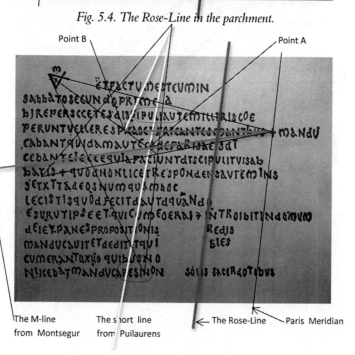

Fig. 5.4. The Rose-Line in the parchment.

Point B   Point A

The M-line   The short line   ← The Rose-Line   Paris Meridian
from Montsegur   from Puilaurens

Fig. 5.5. The Rose-Line with the lines of reflection from Montsegur and
Puilaurens.

47

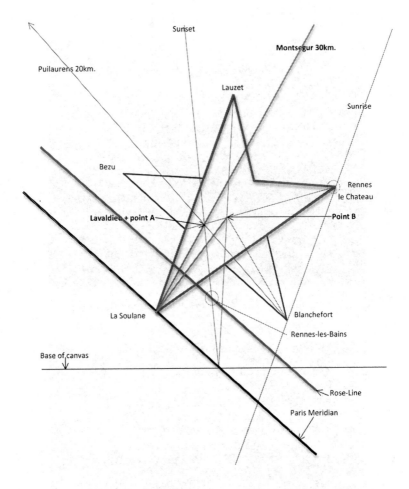

Fig. 5.6. The tip of the spear that pierces Jesus' side with the force of Montsegur.

CHAPTER 3

The Meaning of Poussin and Teniers' Paintings

The secret meaning contained in both Poussin and Teniers' paintings confirms what Gnostics have maintained all along, that it is possible to have a direct experience of God, and by aligning oneself with God, gain access to a divine power that enables one to develop to one's true potential. Both paintings show, in a diagrammatical model form, how it is possible to achieve this through a special way of praying or meditating. This chapter explains the secret meditation technique or prayer that Gnostics performed in order to align themselves with God, and which gave them access to a higher level of consciousness and wisdom.

There are two main barriers to the meditation technique. The first barrier is the lack of a concept to aid one's understanding. Western civilisation has a very head centred perception of the human organism underpinned by the notion that every function that takes place in the human organism has its origin in the brain, the head, our assumed centre of consciousness. Every thought, every action, every emotion, every feeling is conceived as being controlled by the brain. However, this concept does not seem to correspond with our experience of everyday life. Emotions do not seem to fit into this neat little box that is the head centred philosophy. You know emotions, they are those awkward little things that always seem to get in the way of scientific experiments on human behaviour, those inconvenient things that prevent scientists from perfecting artificial intelligence. If scientists could just do away with emotions, they could explain all human behaviour. That is how the human sciences have proceeded in the past, as if human emotions do not exist, behaviourists cannot explain them, so they do their best to ignore them: and yet emotions are the very things that make us most human.

When we experience emotions we do not experience them in our brain, your own experience can confirm this; love is experienced in the heart not the brain, courage, or lack of it, is experienced in the stomach, and responsibility in the shoulders. We have phrases to describe these feelings, we use terms such as being 'warm hearted', 'having guts' or 'no guts', 'having a weight on one's shoulders'. These feelings and emotions are all part of our experience of everyday life, but they do not originate in the brain. The brain may take in the information from the outside world, but it is the whole body that responds with whatever emotional response is appropriate to the situation. The brain receives that emotional information as feedback, that is how I know what I am feeling, but ask me how I am feeling and you might get a different answer. The body has a consciousness all of its own which is apparent when we experience emotions, but a body consciousness is not something that we in the West either recognise or countenance for one moment. Perhaps we are not able to perceive it because we have no concept for it, and without a concept for anything we remain blind to it, and tend to reject and ridicule it, just as we reject and ridicule anything that is incomprehensible to us, and what it is that makes a body consciousness incomprehensible to us is Western philosophy's insistence on a head centred consciousness.

Within Eastern philosophy of human behaviour, the whole body including the head is accepted as being all part of one whole functioning conscious organism. Head and body united in one whole conscious being. A holistic philosophy of psychology opens up new possibilities, new concepts to describe human experience, one that accepts emotions as an integral part of human behaviour. It is revealing that there is not an adequate word in the English language to describe a whole body consciousness, there is no concept for this possibility in everyday usage other than the unwieldy phrase 'mind and body experience'. Jung's term, the psyche, includes both conscious and unconscious aspects of the mind, but which still remains head based. The term psychosoma comes closest, but there is a word that is much more descriptive of the meaning of a whole body consciousness, first used in an open encounter workshop by Will Shutz and Hector Prestera, and later picked up and used by Ken Dychtwald in his book of the same name, *Bodymind*, (1977). The bodymind is a holistic interrelationship of the body and the head, our feelings and our thinking, not separate, they are one whole conscious entity. The pentacle, as illustrated in both Poussin and Teniers' paintings, is symbolic of the bodymind, one whole head and body consciousness. Without the concept of a bodymind, it is difficult to start the meditation technique because there is nothing to work with conceptually.

The second barrier to the secret technique also requires self-knowledge and is the major obstacle to success. Gnostics believe that human beings never fulfil their full potential and remain stunted like withered grapes on the vine. The parable in which Jesus compared Solomon with the lilies of the field has nothing to do with Solomon's fine clothes, which is what I was taught at Sunday school. Solomon was famous for his wisdom, so the parable is comparing the growth of Solomon's wisdom with the lilies' growth, and even as wise as Solomon was, his wisdom had still not grown to its full potential, as the lilies of the field had grown to theirs. The message of this parable is that we all remain stunted spiritual and emotional creatures, unable to grow to our full potential.

What is it then that restricts a person's spiritual and emotional growth and prevents individuals from fulfilling their true potential? When asked this question a Gnostic would always ask you to learn to know yourself. Ask yourself who you are, what is your real self, your true identity? What is it that defines who you are? Is it your job, your status, your circle of friends, your home, your car, the things you own? Is it all of these possessions that define you? What is it that makes all these things its possessions? Are we just our possessions, are we just the things we own? What do you become without those possessions? Who are you when all these things are taken away? The person you believe yourself to be, your identity, is based on your ego's selfish desire and ambition for more and more possessions, and on the social status and power that accrues from that. But all these things can vanish in an instant; what would you be left with? Gnostics believe we have built our self-identities like houses built on sand and as a result, never find our real selves until we are tested. We have invested so much in our egos' self-identity in the mistaken belief that our possessions define us, that we have forgotten who we really are, we have lost touch with ourselves and our souls. Your ego that has developed, your social identity, is not your true identity, it is not the real you, it is an imposter. There is an essence of you, a personal identity, that exists independently of your ego, your social status and your possessions, and it is that part of you that remains undeveloped. But is it not good to have a social identity? We are, after all, social animals. Ideally, our personal identity and our social identity should be one and the same, one whole integrated sense of self, heart and head, feeling and thinking united as one, but our ego head centred thinking has created a social identity devoid of any true feelings at all. Gnostics believe that the ego, the social self, has prospered at the expense of the personal self. We have invested everything in our selfish egos and the desire for more and more possessions, and as a consequence, that ego has become a tyrant that possesses us. Your ego is the biggest obstacle to succeeding with the meditation technique that you will have to face.

Strive hard to know yourself and at finding your true identity. What is it that feels emotion, that laughs, cries, loves, feels emotional pain and joy, gets angry? The life of the emotions is an expression of what your soul feels at a fundamental level. Find that part of yourself that you once knew when you experienced the world unselfconsciously and unashamedly as a child, when your spirit and soul were one and knew no other way of being. The child within you that was separated from you, rejected and disowned long ago.

Definitions: The important key words and phrases.

There are several important elements that form the basis of the meditation technique. The *breath* is extremely important to the whole process because your breath is a link to your inner self. The breath together with the inner light are the keys to performing the technique successfully. *Inner light* is an inner vision, inner sight, the ability to place one's awareness in different parts of the bodymind using the inner eye and the breath to take you there. The *inner eye* is one's sense of self and spiritual essence located behind one's eyes at the brow and activated by one's breath through both nostrils. The line that is dropped down the shaft to find the buried treasure is your inner light from the brow, passing down through the eye of your skull through point A to the heel. *Inner reflection* takes place naturally when the inner light is directed down to the *heels* from the inner eye, the brow, using the breath. The inner light automatically flows back up from the feet, like a reflection. *Libido*, sexual energy, vitality, raw animal energy is also vital to the end result. In the technique, sexual energy is directed inwards, instead of being allowed to follow its natural course and being discharged outwards. *Attention*, concentration on the technique itself and the ability to remain focussed on the task is the most difficult of all the elements to master. One finds oneself distracted all the time and one needs to keep bringing one's attention back to the task in hand. It is the ego that distracts us, always checking our reality, a critical factor always checking what we are doing, self-censoring, keeping us on constant watch. Alchemists compared this element with mercury because like the element mercury, it is difficult to keep hold of and keeps slipping from one's grasp. It is the *honesty* with which one performs the technique that is paramount, throwing one's honest self into the process, *enthusiastically*, with *love, humility and compassion*.

THE BASIC MEDITATION TECHNIQUE or PRAYER

There is one basic meditation technique, but there are three stages to complete the whole process. Each stage of the process uses the basic technique, the only difference being, what one is trying to achieve in each stage. In Poussin's painting, the main reflection **1**, is a natural reflection, from the light source, down to the base of the canvas, and back up to the centre of the pentacle (Fig. 1.10). The natural reflection is symbolic of the inner reflection that has to be performed to complete the technique. The two inner spiritual reflections, **2** and **3**, from the adepts' brows down to the heels and back up to the centre of the pentacle, form the basis of the meditation technique (Fig. 1.10). These three reflections also indicate that there are three stages to complete the process.

Points **A** and **B** in Poussin and Teniers' paintings, (Fig. 1.10), represent two special areas in the bodymind, which can be discovered yourself through practice, by placing your awareness there using the inner light. Thousands of years ago Gnostics in India developed a model in an attempt to understand human spiritual experience. The Chakra system is a model that describes seven energy centres, or centres of consciousness, located at specific points in the body, along the spinal column, progressing upwards from the base chakra at the sacrum, to the crown chakra just above the head (Fig.6.1). Within the Chakra system two centres of consciousness are considered more important than the other five. This distinction is referred to in the Bible in the story of the two loaves and five fishes feeding the ten thousand. This story was not meant to be taken literally, we know it is physically impossible. It was spiritual nourishment that Jesus offered to the masses, not real food. Point **A** corresponds to the water centre in the Chakra system, an area located at the lower navel and associated with the moon. Point **B** corresponds with the upper navel centre in the Chakra system and is associated with the sun.

Play around with and practise the technique of directing your awareness to various parts of your body using your breath to take your inner light there. Experience the emotions and feelings associated with each different part of your body; experience each different level of consciousness. Try seeing with your stomach and experience courage, security, stability and a strong sense of self. Your stomach digests everything and so knows the value of everything and the price of nothing. The loss of contact with this part of your body causes the opposite feelings of fear, anxiety, insecurity, instability and a loss of personal identity. Try to see with your heart and experience love, compassion, tenderness, empathy, and a willingness to reach out to others. The loss of contact with this part of your body can create the inability to love or feel compassion and empathy for anyone, and can lead to a very insular and isolated individual. When you become aware of the emotional responses located in these different parts of your body, then you are experiencing your own bodymind. Practise these exercises until they become second nature to you. Then play around with your breathing; breathe in through your nose whilst trying to experience a sense of self behind your eyes, and experience that level of consciousness. It is as if one is reversing the natural flow of one's sight from outwards to inwards, following the light with one's attention as it flows into one's eyes to an area behind the eyes. One needs to achieve a sense of looking inwards at the same time as looking outwards, gazing inwards and outwards simultaneously. With practice you will be able to experience a strong sense of the essence of your true and honest self here at your inner eye.

Begin the basic meditation technique with a strong sense of your honest self, at a point behind your eyes at your brow, your inner eye. Cast your inner sight, your inner light, down to your water centre, which is point **A** in Poussin's painting (Fig. 1.10) and also point **A** in Fig. 6.2 above, using your inhalation of breath through both nostrils. Gaze through your water centre, point **A**, down to your heels, in an absent-minded, daydream like state, just as the shepherdess in Poussin's painting gazed down through the A in Arcadia down to the

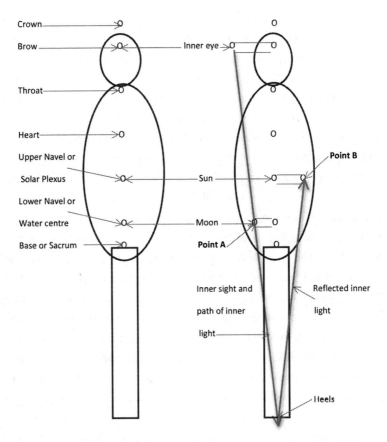

Fig. 6.1. The Chakra system
showing the seven centres of
consciousness.

Fig. 6.2. The basic meditation
technique.

initiate's heel. To assist in this task it can be helpful to gaze into the
embers of a glowing fire, or the flame of a burning candle. The
objective is to look deeper into the embers or beyond the candle with
your gaze, whilst looking deeper within yourself with your inner
light, all the way down to your feet. It also helps if you can do this
with all the enthusiasm you can muster from your shoulders and

your heart. Visualise sending this enthusiasm down to your heels, like an arrow straight and true. All this is to be achieved on the inhalation phase of the full breath cycle. With your awareness now in your feet, as you exhale through your nose, natural good feelings flow up your legs automatically from your feet. Follow this feeling, your inner reflected light, with your inner awareness as it flows back up into your lower navel, point **A**. This absent minded reflective method of the meditation technique is the only way to avoid your ego's eye, your ego's constant critical censorship of what you are doing. With all those good feelings in your lower navel the objective now is to focus all this natural energy at one small point in the centre of your bodymind in the upper navel, the solar plexus, point **B**. It can help to focus the energy at this point with love or sadness, but especially with honest humility, being your true and humble self. From your upper navel centre, point **B**, on each exhalation, visualise sending out this energy from your sun centre through your limbs to the far reaches of the solar system as if reaching out. Imagine being connected in this way to the entire universe. Your sun centre shines out in the spiritual universe, a star is born.

The basic technique, in itself, is nothing new, there are similar techniques taught in meditation seminars today. The difference with this technique is the knowledge of what is achievable, and faith in the eventual outcome and the objective of the technique. Each of the three stages of the meditation technique is defined by a specific colour that best describes the objective in that stage. The colours of each stage in the order they are achieved are: Stage 1—Black, Stage 2—White and Stage 3—Red. By now hopefully, you will have come to the conclusion that your ego is not the real you and is expendable, because the first stage of the process is all about death; the death of the ego.

STAGE 1: The death of the ego—Black

I would like to make it quite clear from the start that this stage does not involve the physical death of anyone. If any person harms themselves or anyone else after reading this book, then they have misunderstood what I have written. The examples I give are not to be taken literally. This stage is about an inner death, the death of one form of consciousness, ego consciousness, for another.

This is the most difficult stage to pass through because the ego does not want to give up its existence. But your ego is not you, your ego is an imposter, your Gemini twin, it is Jesus' twin brother Doubting Thomas. Your ego is not your real self, it is expendable for a greater good. You may disagree that your ego is not who you are, because you have so much invested in it. After all, your ego has always been there for you, defended you against others, protected you, looked after your interests, looked after number one, defined you as an individual within the wider group. Your ego is your best friend, surely? And yet your ego restricts you, your ego censures you, your ego limits your ability, your ego doubts you, your ego is a control freak, your ego thinks it is the boss of you, your ego even thinks it possesses you. The ego has always protected you from the vagaries of the outside world, like a thick skin, but it is exactly that tough exterior that eventually restricts our spiritual growth, and just like the spider, the snake, the crab and the scorpion, one has to cast off that ego skin, that ego armour, in a spiritual sense, in order to grow to one's true potential. There is no easy way around this, your ego has to die. You have to persuade your ego that it has to lay down its life for you. This is the real meaning of the words in the Bible, "no man hath a greater friend than one who lays down his life for you", it was this dilemma that the Bible was referring to. Your ego is not about to go quietly, it will do anything to avoid its demise, it may even tell you this book is a load of old rubbish. This of course could be true, but in any event, this may be a long process of self-discovery before you even attempt the first stage. What helps in the process of ridding yourself of your ego is to take away its life blood, all of its possessions. You must be prepared to give up everything you possess and reject everything you believe to be true. The poor have a distinct advantage over the rich in this respect, they have nothing to lose, so the first shall be last and the last shall be first. Your ego has to give up its life in good faith, it must come to recognise that it has to make way for something better to come. Your ego has to want to die for a greater good and because it knows that it is the right thing to do for you. You must have faith in this greater good, you must do this for yourself.

This is your Indiana Jones moment when he stepped off the ledge into the abyss. This is the ultimate test of your faith, you have to step off that spiritual ledge into the spiritual abyss, with only my reassurance to guide you. God will not let you fall or descend into madness as your ego fears.

The spirit behind your eyes, the inner eye at the brow, is the Daemon Guardian at midday in parchment four, your own personal shepherdess or shepherd, your guardian angel. In Jesus' time, Gnostics would have compared the ego to a demon that possesses people. Jesus was attributed with the ability to cast out demons, but he did not cast out demons from other people, it's impossible. He cast the demon out of himself, the demon that possessed him was his own possessive ego. The objective of stage one is to kill your ego, to exorcise that demon, and cast off, shed, the ego skin, the ego shell, the ego armour that confines you.

Begin stage one with the basic technique by casting your inner light down to your heels, but this time focus the reflected light through both navel centres up to the heart centre. Focus all the energy at your heart centre with sadness, with a sense of loss and heartache, and with suffering. Empty your heart completely, reject everything you have ever been taught or believed to be true, wipe the slate clean. Open your heart up to the universe. Let go of everything you think is you. Create a vacuum in your heart, a void. Nature abhors a vacuum, and will fill it with new truths based on the wisdom of the ages, the Wisdom of the Universe, perhaps Jung's archetypes.

The story of Achilles relates to stage one of the process. Achilles was a great hero in Greek mythology, who was invincible in battle because of his armour. His suit of armour covered him from head to foot, protecting him completely from mortal blows. But it was an arrow that killed him when it struck him at the one place the armour did not protect, his heel. It was not Achilles that died though, it was his ego, and the one that fired the arrow was Achilles' own spirit, his true and honest self. His armour symbolises a powerful and impregnable ego that was brought down by an arrow, symbol of the inner light flying straight and true, carried through the air, symbol of the breath to its target, the heel (Fig. 6.3).

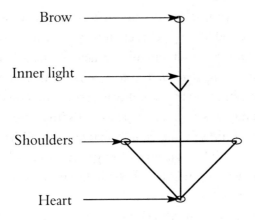

Fig. 6.3. The arrow that killed Achilles.

In time your ego will fade away, but your real self will continue, your essence will survive. You will not have lost touch with reality as your ego feared, but your reality will have changed, you will have changed for ever, but you will be free to grow to a new level of development, a much wiser level, a higher form of consciousness. You may feel vulnerable for a time, until your new ego skin hardens, as a new ego develops, which again will subsequently limit your growth, but this time, you will know who the boss is and will tolerate your new ego as long as it serves your purpose. Your ego is like a wild animal that needs taming. Once you have completed stage one, you will have tamed your beast and it will do your bidding from now on. This tamed animal is the 'Horse of God' referred to in parchment four, and the reins steering, guiding, controlling your horse of God is the breath through each nostril, connected to your horse by the inner light. Your horse of God is also Pegasus from Greek mythology.

The story of Perseus in Greek mythology also relates to stage one of the process. Perseus killed Medusa armed only with a sword and a mirrored shield. By looking at the reflection of Medusa in his shield, Perseus was able to avoid looking at her directly and being turned to stone. The mirrored shield is a symbol for the reflective process, and the sword, the same as the arrow, is the symbol for air, a symbol for the breath and the inner light. So, with his breath and inner reflected light Perseus was able to kill Medusa, his own ego. Both these Greek myths of Achilles and Perseus are Gnostic scriptures, told to their initiates as an introduction to the spiritual process.

STAGE 2: Purification—White

Stage two is the preparation for the final stage. The purification process is a cleansing of the body on the inside using the inner light like water, and as a means of creating a little heat to burn off impurities. Internal impurities in the bodymind are caused by muscular tensions that prevent the free flow of emotions and feelings. Muscular tensions are created by your ego in an attempt to protect itself, by holding on to its reality, and to prevent it and you from feeling too much emotional pain. The ego does this by restricting the natural free flow of emotions by contracting certain muscles and suppressing others. Over time, muscular tensions and suppressions become fixed into a type of character armour, revealed in a persistent way of responding, and attitude to the world (Reich, 1972). Personality revealed in a fixed way of holding one's body, in how one sets one's body to defend against emotional pain, leading to a muscular stance against the world revealed in musculature holding patterns. This is the real language of the body, e.g. a person with a protruding lower jaw who was continually frustrated as a child, perhaps by overbearing parents. As a child they learnt to ward off feelings of anger and wanting to shout at their parents by defiantly sticking out their lower jaw. This action may have overcome the initial crisis by suppressing the act of wanting to shout out angrily, but over time, that action became a consistent and persistent approach to any form of frustration. The continuous suppression of the act of wanting to rage against unfairness becomes fixed in the jaw. Observing someone with a protruding lower jaw would give one the impression of somebody who is very stubborn and determined to get their own way, despite their parents. The opposite of this type of holding pattern is the chinless wonder, someone with no resolve at all. Try sticking out your own lower jaw and see how it makes you feel. Then there are the people we see on the beach, whose upper body and lower body do not seem to belong to each other. There is the well-developed, sometimes obese upper body, with sparrow's legs, then there is the well-developed lower body with tin ribs. These are two extremes of the upper and lower body split, which generally equate with extroversion in the well-developed upper body and introversion in the well-developed lower body. They have both filled out, developed those parts of their personalities as revealed in their body shape. The extrovert has developed the ability to reach out socially with the upper body and the introvert's lower body has developed out of the need to feel grounded and secure. There are many more fixed holding patterns manifested in the human body, unique to each individual, but each one indicative of a specific emotional blockage and a distinctive type of attitude to the world (Dychtwald, 1977). I would also recommend taking up the practise of Yoga during stage two of the process. You may have rid yourself of your ego, but your ego's legacy lives on in your musculature, your distinctive holding pattern. Regular gentle stretching of the muscles breaks down your ego's character armour and prevents any further build up. In performing these stretching exercises, Yoga also opens up and frees your emotional energy channels. The objective of stage two is to cleanse and purify your inner body, your bodymind, and to remove the remnants of the ego skin, ego shell, ego armour, in preparation for stage three of the process.

Stage two begins with the basic technique, casting your inner light down to your feet. This time follow the reflected light up into your legs, experiencing good feelings in your thighs and hips. Keep the awareness of those good feelings and by increasing the rate of your breathing, exaggerate those feelings. Build this process up to a climax using your breathing like Alchemists' bellows, creating a gentle heat in your thighs and hips, until all the tension in your body is forced out of every pore of your body, like escaping smoke or steam. If you perform this task properly, there will be a distinctive aroma exuded from every pore of your body.

There is a second part to stage two of the process which Taoists describe as the circulation of the light. Begin the second part of stage two with the basic technique, casting your inner light down to your feet. This time, in following the reflected light back up your bodymind, visualise the energy flowing up to your heart, branching out to both shoulders, and then flowing down your arms, and back to your feet again in a continuous loop. This exercise helps to cleanse and keep open your emotional energy channels.

The practice by Muslims of washing their feet five times a day was not meant to be taken literally. Muslims should be cleansing their feet spiritually with the inner light acting as water. Washing feet with real water is only symbolic of a spiritual exercise. Likewise, the practice of baptism, being immersed in water to symbolise spiritual rebirth, was also not meant to be taken literally. Water is just symbolic of the inner light with which one immerses oneself on the inside to achieve spiritual rebirth.

Templars were accused by their inquisitors of trampling and

spitting on the cross, which they could not deny, but trampling or spitting on the cross to them means something completely different to what one would think. This is the way of Gnostics, to make the meaning the exact opposite to what the unknowing would believe. Trampling or spitting on the cross to the unknowing would indicate a sign of a lack of respect for the cross and by association the entire Christian religion, it was viewed as blasphemous. This is the literal interpretation of the verb 'to trample', but Gnostics were referring to their spiritual interpretation of that verb, which is to clean, to whiten, to purify, as one would do when washing clothes in those days, by trampling on them in a washtub. To trample on the cross to a Gnostic means to purify the spiritual body, the bodymind, as is to spit on the cross in order to polish it as in 'spit and polish', just another act of cleansing.

STAGE 3: The Holy Grail—Red

Teniers' painting uses the eye of the skull and the base of the crucifix to indicate the same two points as Poussin's painting, point A the moon centre, and point B the sun centre, conveniently placing a candle holder by the side of the skull as an indication of how to proceed. There are two extra features in Teniers' painting, both relevant to stage three of the process. These are the two birds and the jar on the far left of the painting. The two birds are illustrating something that comes to us from the air. It has already been described as bread of heaven or manna from God. The painting is trying to tell us something about the air we breathe into our body. Rosicrucians referred to themselves as 'brothers of the boiled dew'. They described a substance that behaved like morning dew collecting on the grass, something that condenses out of the air we breathe. A substance invisible in the air, but contained within the air that was extremely valuable to them. Teniers' painting is telling us there is something contained in the air we breathe, that sustains us and nourishes us spiritually. The jar on the left is just symbolic of the Holy Grail. Gnostics believe that the physical world we see around us is an illusion and that ultimate reality is a spiritual reality. They believe the physical world derives its existence from something akin to a spiritual template. Plato alluded to this possibility in the analogy of a group of people chained to the wall of a cave, and who had only ever seen the shadows on the wall of the cave, cast by the light from a fire. What these people see on the cave walls, the shadows cast by the fire, becomes their reality, whereas reality is the object moving in front of the fire, casting its shadow on the wall. Plato's cave analogy is a good description of the relationship that may exist between physical reality and spiritual reality. What we see as our physical reality could be just the shadow of a spiritual reality. I accept that the next paragraph is pure speculation, but it is a justifiable attempt to make sense of the new revelation in the paintings, and a real experience.

It may be that for every human function there is a spiritual equivalent. Our physical body could have a spiritual equivalent, as the bodymind I have described, and as the Chakra system illustrates in diagrammatical form. Our physical form may derive, just like the shadow, from our spiritual form as Plato's cave analogy suggests. The human cardio-vascular and respiratory systems may also have a spiritual equivalent. The air we breathe and the oxygen contained in it may have spiritual equivalents. The heart may have a spiritual equivalent, it could be the heart centre indicated by the Chakra system. Just as re-oxygenated blood keeps us alive and invigorates the physical body so it could be that the spiritual equivalent of re-oxygenated blood invigorates the spiritual body and keeps that alive also. This of course may not be what actually happens, but it does help in carrying out the process to visualise it this way. If there is such a spiritual circulatory system, then that described in stage three of the process may be the beginning of it.

Stage three begins with the basic technique, but this time summon up all the honesty and sincerity in your heart and upper body and cast that down with your inner sight through your moon centre to your feet. Whatever it is in the air that may be the spiritual equivalent of oxygen, let's call it spirit, condenses when it comes into contact with libido, emotional and sexual energy, your spiritual haemoglobin, let's call it soul. Spirit and soul combined to create a new substance that facilitates a spiritual circulatory system. Your emotions are your soul's blood supply, your spirit is what invigorates it. The new substance, the spiritual equivalent of re-oxygenated blood, is the dew of Rosicrucians, the mercury of Alchemists that turns to gold, Reich's orgone and Kundalini in the Chakra system. This new substance flows up to the sun centre at the upper navel, where it is focussed at that small point in the centre of the bodymind, point B in Poussin and Teniers' paintings, where it is focussed and squeezed through a tiny channel that links the sun centre to the heart centre, using the utmost sincerity to keep focussed. Continue this process with each succeeding breath until you begin to feel your chest filling up with liquid goodness. Eventually, you will begin to feel pressure growing at your shoulders as your chest fills to its maximum, and all those liquid feelings reach that level. Then suddenly, the pressure is released, as all those good feelings flow down your arms like a warm internal fluid. Your spiritual circulation has commenced and envelopes you in a warm, contented glow, a cocoon like state of wholeness. Your cup truly hath run over.

It is well-known to followers of the mystery of Rennes le Chateau, and it has been discussed many times previously by experts on the subject, the French word for Holy Grail is *sangreal*, but in old French it was separated thus, *san greal*. The transposition of the letter G gives *sang real* or blood royal, royal blood (Fig. 6.4).

FRENCH		ENGLISH
SAN GREAL	–	HOLY GRAIL
SANG REAL	–	ROYAL BLOOD

Fig. 6.4.

As we have seen, this simple play on words is the typical hallmark of a Gnostic at work. The secret placed right in front of our eyes, but at the same time hidden. The observation in Fig. 6.4 led Baigent, Leigh and Lincoln (1986) to conclude that a royal blood that was holy, must belong to Jesus Christ, and therefore, the holy bloodline must be Jesus' direct descendants. The hypothesis they arrived at in their book, *Holy Blood and the Holy Grail*, was that the mystery of Rennes le Chateau contained the revelation that there is a holy bloodline descending directly from Jesus through Mary Magdalene and exists to this day in secret. Dan Brown also had a best-selling novel based on this premise (2003), but the holy bloodline hypothesis was just another red herring.

The Holy Grail is not a royal or holy bloodline. The Holy Grail is indeed a receptacle, and a receptacle for containing royal or holy blood, but the Holy Grail is not a physical object and the royal holy blood is not real blood. Royal holy blood is available to all of us; this is a royal holy blood that can flow through everyone's spiritual veins. Royal holy blood is the same substance produced by stage three of the meditation technique. A spiritual substance that condenses out of the air we breathe to combine with our emotional and sexual energy, our vitality, to produce a new substance, royal and holy blood. Once it is produced by stage three of the process, royal and holy blood percolates up to the sun centre, where it passes through the eye of the needle to the heart centre, where, symbolically, it acts like a spear piercing the heart, which symbolically bleeds, filling the receptacle in our spiritual chest. The spiritual receptacle located in our spiritual chest is the Holy Grail and the substance that fills it is royal and holy blood. The Holy Grail is the receptacle and the royal holy blood it contains. The Holy Grail also refers to the whole process (Fig. 6.5).

This is the pirate treasure you seek, a treasure that was there for you all along, contained in your chest, your 'treasure chest' of course, those Gnostic rascals! The parable about a camel having more chance of passing through the eye of a needle than a rich man has of entering the Kingdom of God refers to stage three of the process. The camel represents the tamed animal energy carried on the reflected light, and the eye of the needle is that tiny point, which leads to the passageway, the gates of heaven through which it has to be squeezed, to reach the heart. Le Pique in the landscape can now be seen in symbolic terms as the eye of the needle, reaching out to God. Le Pique is the most holiest of locations in the world, reaching out to God on a horizontal as well as a vertical plane as all true churches should. In reaching the heart centre, one really is entering the Kingdom of God. Royal and Holy Blood is the substance produced in stage three of the meditation process, it is the same substance as Kundalini, as Rosicrucian's dew, orgone and Alchemists' mercury. There is another feature of the Holy Grail that proves its authenticity; Gnostics were able to drink from the Holy Grail because only they knew how to fill it, traditionally the Holy Grail is the only chalice that fills from the stem. Completion of stage three of the process, drinking from the Holy Grail, bestows on one immortality.

The meaning contained in Poussin and Teniers' paintings, in Henry Lincoln's pentacle in the landscape and the secret of Rennes le Chateau, is the revelation that the Holy Grail is a real phenomenon, and the paintings show how it is possible to gain access to it by way of a secret meditation technique or method of prayer. The secret is not a physical treasure, but a spiritual treasure, just as Plantard said. This treasure is there for all of us, it is a gift from God, the gift of one's immortal self. Only you have to take it, nobody can do it for you. You have to open the door yourself. You have the key to do it now. Only you can open the door (Figs. 6.6 and 6.7).

As a general overview of the objective of the whole spiritual process, the terms spirit and soul are a good example of the sense of oneness that is achievable. The terms spirit and soul are often used interchangeably as if describing the same thing. They are actually polar but complementary opposites described in Gnostic literature

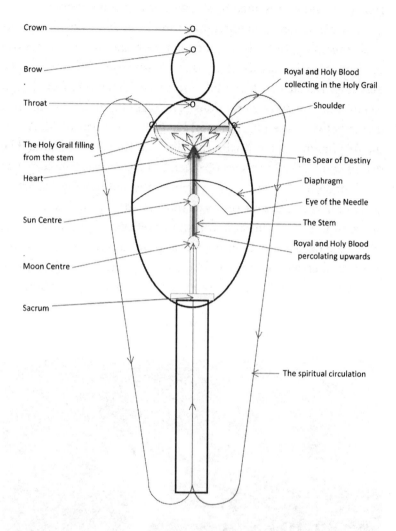

Crown

Brow

Throat

Royal and Holy Blood
collecting in the Holy Grail

Shoulder

The Holy Grail filling
from the stem

The Spear of Destiny

Heart

Diaphragm

Eye of the Needle

Sun Centre

The Stem

Royal and Holy Blood
percolating upwards

Moon Centre

Sacrum

The spiritual circulation

Fig. 6.5. The Holy Grail and Royal and Holy Blood. The spiritual circulation.

as sun and moon, king and queen, salt and sulphur, prince and princess, the lion and the lamb, Adam and Eve, Yin and Yang. The soul is associated with the lower body, below the diaphragm, and centred in the lower navel, the water centre of the chakra system

(Fig. 6.8), and represented by a downward pointing triangle.

The diaphragm is an interesting muscle, not only does it regulate one's breathing, but it is also the main tool the ego uses to control our emotional responses, by suppressing our breathing. The diaphragm is shaped like a lid, and that is exactly its function, it 'keeps a lid' on all our emotions. The diaphragm is also the great divide between the physical world and the spiritual world. Above the diaphragm, in spiritual terms, lies the Kingdom of God. The diaphragm not only acts as a barrier, but also as the gatekeeper to this kingdom. The diaphragm is, physically and literally, the actual 'gates of heaven', and the only way through those gates is stage three of the process, by squeezing your inner reflected light through the eye of the needle, symbolically like a spear, to pierce your spiritual heart , and create the royal and holy blood. Before the Holy Grail, Gnostics used Gabriel's Horn to refer to the secret process in just

Fig. 6.6. The Holy Grail hidden in 'The Shepherds of Arcadia II'.

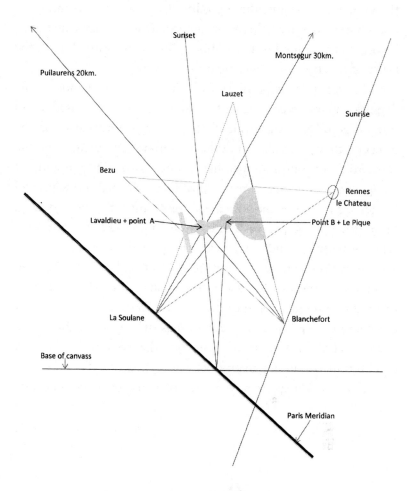

Fig. 6.7 The Holy Grail hidden in the landscape.

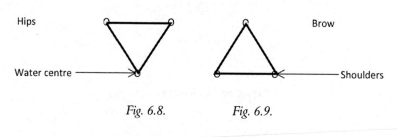

Fig. 6.8.   *Fig. 6.9.*

the same way, e.g. something produced out of the air (sound), by one's breath, that has to pass through a narrow passage (the horn), before it is amplified to make music. So when Joshua fought the battle of Jericho, '*the walls* came tumbling down'.

The spirit is associated with the upper body above the diaphragm, and is centred in the brow and is represented by an upward pointing triangle (Fig. 6.9). These two forces strive in the direction they point, the soul to feel grounded and secure, and the spirit to reach out and soar like a bird. Two opposite and yet complementary natures contained within us, the male principle and the female principle, the anima and the animus, the yin and yang. Stage three of the process unites these opposing forces into one sense of harmony and wholeness. Using the basic technique, the spirit is cast down from the brow to the feet, and reflected back up to unite with the soul located in the moon centre. The spirit then lifts the soul up to the sun centre where it is fixed at the centre of the bodymind, point B in the paintings, which is the eye of the needle. The spirit lifts and supports the soul in a balanced equilibrium, combining to produce a new sense of self at the centre of the bodymind, your new centre of consciousness. The two

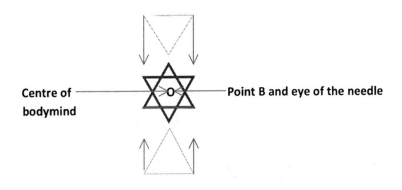

Centre of bodymind ———————— Point B and eye of the needle

Fig.6.10.The star of David.

triangles lock together to form an emblem of wholeness and symbol of oneness with God, as the Star of David (Fig. 6.10). For a male it means embracing the feminine side of his nature and for a female embracing the masculine side of hers.

The human skeleton has always been used by Gnostics as a symbol for the human spirit because just as the skeleton supports the flesh, so the spirit supports the soul. You can perhaps now see why the skull and crossbones is so important to Rosicrucians, and is another example of the way Gnostics, in their immense wisdom, utilise a reversal of reality to emphasise their point; the skull and crossbones appearing to be superficially a symbol of evil, but in actual fact the exact opposite, and presented in this way in order to ward off the ignorant and the superstitious whilst simultaneously giving a subtle message.

Gnostics have a wonderful grasp of the psychology and dynamics of the bodymind, they are alone in that field and they play around effortlessly, flipping with ease from a spiritual to a literal meaning. Most of their stories are designed to highlight the inner conflict between the real self, and its attempts to grow spiritually, and the ego that does not want to change at all. Their stories are about how our ego alienates us from ourselves and in doing so from God also. Those fairy tales about the princess locked away in the ivory tower, held prisoner there by the wicked queen, were Gnostic stories to describe the relationship that exists between the ego and the personal self, the soul. The prince, as spirit, rescues the princess' soul from the wicked ego's control, and only after that were they able to live happily ever after, united in one dynamic bodymind.

Snow White and the Seven Dwarves is a fairy tale with lots of secret symbolism. The seven dwarves represent the seven chakras, they mined down a hole in the ground, so their working environment was often filled with gold and precious gems. The wicked queen had a mirror on the wall with which she consulted the reflected light, a reflection that seemed to prefer Snow White's beauty. And each attempt by the queen to kill Snow White's soul was thwarted by the dwarves (chakras) who brought her spirit back to life again. Similarly, in Cinderella, the stepmother and the two ugly sisters are facets of Cinderella's ego, and the glass slipper is a reference to reflected light from the feet, which helps the prince to find her and thwart the stepmother.

In the Bible, Eve was the true heroine of the Garden of Eden. Eve's spirit rescued Adam's soul from the jealous, angry, vengeful god of the Old Testament, Adam's ego. The serpent represents Eve's wisdom, and the Tree of Life which Eve persuaded Adam to eat the fruit from, is the Sephiroth, a mystic system similar to the Chakra system, used by the Kabbalah, a Gnostic branch of Judaism. This angry, jealous god of the Old Testament is the Gnostic false god, the ego that knows no other god but itself. But in this story, Eve fails to kill Adam's ego and they are thus both thrown out of the Garden of Eden, i.e. the bodymind, and separated from each other again.

Gnostics observed the world around them and saw nature in the raw. They took examples from nature to describe the spiritual process because they could see that process reflected in nature. One analogy they took from a natural human function that they used to describe and represent stage three of the process was the physical birth of a baby, from conception through gestation, to birth. In this analogy the water or moon centre, the spiritual womb, is the exact equivalent of the physical womb. The breath of God, our inner light, our spiritual breath, moves on the face of the water centre. Spirit and soul enjoy spiritual intercourse, sexual energy being directed inwards, and a spiritual child is conceived in the spiritual womb. The spiritual foetus is nourished in the spiritual womb by the circulation of the light producing bread of heaven, and the foetus grows until it is ready to be born. But the birth of a spiritual baby takes place in the opposite direction to a phyical birth. The spiritual birth canal is the narrow passage between the sun centre and the heart centre, the eye of the needle. A new spiritual baby has been born and its cradle is the heart centre, a manger where the Horse of

God feeds. This is the rebirth of the soul. A new spiritual being has been created and takes its place in the spiritual universe, as an immortal soul.

Templars were accused by their inquisitors of burning babies, which they could not deny. How they loved to tease the unknowing, it became an art form, but which eventually backfired on them with tragic consequences not only for themselves, but for the whole of humanity. This phrase was not meant to be taken literally, burning babies is a reference to the gentle heat applied to the newly born spiritual baby in the heart in order to create the Holy Grail, it's just another different analogy for the same process, it's a combination of the virgin birth and the Alchemist's bellows. It is also possible now to see that trampling on the cross was not only to purify the spiritual body, but also to produce wine by treading the grapes, the chakras.

CHAPTER 4

The Implications of the Meaning in Poussin and Teniers' Paintings

A secret wisdom has existed from the earliest civilisations and been handed down to each succeeding generation of Gnostics. Gnostics claim to know God and it is reasonable to assume that the Great Secret is concerned with this knowledge. What secret knowledge could be any greater than this? Gnostics have kept the secret alive in their writing, in stories, in mysteries and in parables. This was the way they taught their new initiates, with these stories that were designed to highlight the secret wisdom. The secret wisdom was almost eradicated by the Catholic Church, but Gnosticism and the secret wisdom survived and exists incognito in secret organisations to this day. Gnostics continued to encode the secret wisdom in their written work, some of which became recognised as great works of literature. Mysteries in particular highlighted the paradox of something that can be a hoax and not a hoax at the same time depending on a literal or spiritual interpretation of events, this being one of the hallmarks of Gnostic writing. One great mystery that has this feature is that of Rennes le Chateau, and despite numerous forgeries, bogus organisations and red herrings, it was the paintings by Poussin and Teniers that are the focal point of the mystery. Both paintings contain the secret in graphic detail, which has now appeared for the first time in the public domain, so there can be no doubt about its existence, but what it means is open to interpretation. My interpretation is that the paintings reveal the secret knowledge, which is a meditation technique or prayer that allows one to have a direct experience of God, just as Gnostics have always maintained, but, furthermore, access to God allows one to develop to a much higher spiritual level, attaining the Holy Grail and through that, spiritual immortality. The barriers that prevent one from reaching a higher level of consciousness are a lack of self-awareness and the way the ego defends itself, being the biggest obstacle to the process one has to face. Another obstacle is the lack of a concept to grasp the meaning, and the notion of a bodymind bridged the gap between Western head centred philosophy and the secret process that allows the mental leap to become possible. There are three stages to the meditation technique and I have given examples from Gnostic writing that were relevant to each stage. I also gave examples in models and analogies to clarify the whole process and in doing so raised the possibility of the existence of a spiritual template for the physical body which suggests our cardio-vascular and respiratory circulatory systems are based on a spiritual circulatory system. I also suggested there is a substance in the spiritual air we breathe that combines with our emotional and sexual vitality to produce a special substance, Royal and Holy Blood, which can be collected in a special spiritual receptacle located in the chest which is the Holy Grail. Drinking from the Holy Grail confers on one spiritual immortality, that is my faith.

I introduced several concepts along the way to illustrate the points I have been making, some of which are not new concepts. All I have done is to bring all these concepts and models together in a new synthesis based on the new knowledge in an attempt to make sense of a bigger picture. Models, by their very nature, can never be the whole truth, especially when trying to explain spiritual truth. They only approximate the truth until a new model comes along that explains the truth more clearly and then the first model is discarded. That is how science and knowledge have always proceeded, e.g. the Earth was considered to be the centre of the universe until Copernicus pointed out that the Earth actually orbits the sun. The models, concepts and analogies I have used are also approximate truths, attempts to understand the nature of an invisible reality, how our spiritual and emotional experience behaves and interacts with our physical experience. I introduced graphic visible examples and models of what is fundamentally an invisible spiritual process. Some may reject the notion of an invisible reality or a science based on an invisible concept yet readily accept the existence of the mind and consciousness because we experience those ourselves, we are aware of their existence even though we cannot see them, and we already have one such working model based on an invisible reality that is recognised as a science and accepted throughout the world, the psychodynamic model of human behaviour based on the work of Freud and the post Freudians. In the end the concepts I have presented are just tentative working models devised in the light of the new revelations in Poussin and Teniers' paintings, hypotheses about how our visible physical existence and the invisible spiritual and emotional experience might inter-relate and interact with one another. We already have several candidates now for how the ghost may be able to exist within the machine; the debate should perhaps move on to how the ghost may be able to exist without the machine.

New concepts open up the possibility of new insights leading to fresh ideas. The concept of a truly holistic notion of the human organism, the bodymind, with the centre of a spiritual and emotional conscious mind, our sense of being, located at the sun centre, the tip of the solar plexus, the eye of the needle, the centre of the bodymind, point B in the paintings, instead of a head centred consciousness is as revolutionary as Copernicus' notion of a sun centred solar system. The bodymind concept of a sun centred consciousness, supported by the meaning contained in Poussin and Teniers' paintings is revolutionary; it moves the goalposts, turns everything on its head. This is a whole new ball game, opening up a whole range of new possibilities. The implications of this revelation are potentially enormous on several different levels, for religion, for psychology, psychiatry and mental health, socially, politically and academically.

The implication for Rennes le Chateau is that the mystery is solved and we can move on from that now and concentrate on what emerged from it. In retrospect, it can be seen that it was only the paintings and Lincoln's pentacle in the landscape that were important and everything else surrounding the mystery was a means to that end. There never was a hidden physical treasure, the secret was a hidden spiritual treasure just as Plantard had said. Saunière probably made his money selling the secret to wealthy people. Professor Cornford's pentagon was wrong because he could not conceive the centre of it being anything other than the head of the shepherdess. He could not see that, because of a head centred obsession we all share in the West. The pentagon and pentacle were there alright, just as Lincoln had been informed, but one had to throw away mind-forged manacles to see it. The holy bloodline was a red herring because Baigent et al. could not conceive of any holy royal blood not belonging to Jesus Christ and his descendants. There never was a holy bloodline. Why would that have been important anyway? Why would descendants of Jesus be any more important than anyone else? Would we have wanted to worship them too? There are no bones of Jesus buried under Mount Cardou, this was another red herring. Why would these have been important anyway? Would we even worship bones? Why do we worship things, objects and icons, instead of ideals, values and principles? Why do we worship Jesus on the cross, a crucifix, and ignore the ideals, values and principles he is supposed to have lived and died for?

Implications for Religion

The enormous implications for both Catholic Religion and Protestant Religion is that they are not needed anymore. The sole purpose of religion should have been to help and teach people how to grow closer to God. Self-knowledge leading to the meditation technique outlined, a special way of praying, was what the Christian Church was supposed to be teaching us, but somewhere along the line that message got lost and we literally ended up with the blind leading the blind. The first council of Nicaea was the final nail in the coffin of spiritual truth, and ever since then, the Catholic and subsequently Protestant Churches have been misleading their followers. We do not need religion anymore because not only will it continue to mislead people, but also, now that we know the secret method of prayer, we can cut out the middle man, the Church, bishops and priests, and deal directly with God ourselves, as it always should have been. We do not need spiritual leaders to tell us what to do, we can do it ourselves now that we have the means to do so. Each and every one of us is responsible for our own salvation.

Jesus was a good man, a role model, a man who stood up for the poor and oppressed, who was not motivated by greed or money, who was not competitive or aggressive, but stood up to authority when he saw injustice taking place. This is a man who I have always respected and admired, so it has been difficult for me to come to the conclusion, from the evidence, that Jesus may never have existed at all as a real person, and that he was probably just a figment of a Gnostic storyteller's imagination.

I am not the first person to suggest that Jesus was not a real person, Madam Blavatsky (1877), in volume II of *Isis Unveiled*, Roy Norvill (1986, pp 128 and 240), and more recently, Freke and Gandy (1999, pp 120-4), pointed out the similarities between the story of Jesus and other religious, pagan and mythical figures from history. Horus/Osiris in Egypt, Dionysius in Greece, Zoroaster and Mithras in Persia, Krishna and Buddha in Asia. All these heroes have similar life stories, born of a virgin in a cave or cowshed, turned water into wine, rode into town on a donkey whilst people waved palm leaves to honour him, died at Easter as a sacrifice for the sins of the world, rose from the dead after three days, baptised followers who await his return on the day of judgement, his death celebrated ritually with bread and wine to symbolise his body and blood. Most of these religious leaders' stories are considerably older than Jesus', predating it by hundreds even thousands of years, so Jesus' story is not even the original story. These legendary myths are based on the original greatest story ever told, written by a Gnostic scribe, hundreds of years before Jesus was born, borrowed from, and plagiarised down the ages, and re-issued anew for each generation with just a name change for the central figure, the hero.

So why should Jesus be any more special than all these other religious heroes, and why should all these other figures' stories be false and just the Jesus story true? They cannot all be literally true, it would be a miracle if all these religious leaders had almost identical life stories, and if one is considered to be false then all are suspect. Unless of course one uses the theological argument of 'anticipatory plagiarism by the devil', which entails the devil having written all these prior stories in order to undermine Jesus' later coming. It is nonsense, of course, but this is the sort of contorted logic and supernatural illusion one has to accept in order to continue to believe that Jesus was a real person.

There is one possibility that Jesus was a real person. Sometimes Gnostics wove their message around real people and events, and Jesus could have been one such good man who did good deeds and who lived in Jerusalem at the right time' and around whose life Gnostics saw the opportunity to weave the traditional story. But that would also mean that Jesus was just an ordinary man and not the actual son of God at all.

The story of Jesus is central to all Christian religions. Christians believe that the story of Jesus in the New Testament is an accurate representation of his life, but there is a problem with the story. A big gap exists between the infant Jesus and the adult Jesus, with nothing in between, except one short story of him as a twelve year old turning up at the synagogue, after which all the priests remarked how spiritually advanced he was for his age. This does not sound very convincing evidence that the event actually took place, it just sounds like someone's attempt to fill in those embarrassing missing years, because in it, nothing remarkable happens, and in the event, just what everyone would expect church leaders to say about the future Messiah. But there could be a good reason for this gap in years if Jesus never existed as a real person, because childhood and teenage years do not lend themselves well at all as being symbolic of the spiritual process that Jesus represents.

The life story of Jesus in the New Testament has been portrayed by two different analogies separated in time by those gap years. The first analogy relates to the birth of Jesus. In the Orthodox Christian version of this event we are expected to believe in an immaculate conception, that Mary conceived a child without having had sexual intercourse with a man; but not only that, Mary had never had sexual intercourse with any man ever, not even her husband, and remained a virgin. This is the kind of medieval and superstitious religious belief that we have to see beyond and leave behind if we are to enter a new spiritual age in the 21st century. As rational people we know that an immaculate conception is physically impossible. So we are left with two possibilities, the literal interpretation of events, which would inevitably lead one to the conclusion that the whole of the Christian faith is based on Mary's infidelity and the story she told Joseph when he found out, or this whole event was meant to be interpreted spiritually. The Orthodox insistence on a literal interpretation of this event leaves them with the problem of Mary's adultery. If one follows the logic of the Church's literal interpretation of events and accept that Joseph had no carnal knowledge of Mary, then the inevitable conclusion is that Mary had to have committed adultery, but then the Church pulls off a neat trick by introducing the Holy Ghost in order to get around this problem. But the Holy Ghost cannot produce sperm; it is supposed to be pure spirit. Either way Joseph has still been cuckolded by God. What sort of a god is this? And don't you think that Joseph is entitled to feel a little bit hacked off, to put it mildly? Was he even consulted? But no, he remains the kind, supportive, understanding and forgiving husband that in these circumstances, definitely does not exist. It is all quite nonsensical of course, but it is a nonsense created by a literal interpretation of this event. The Christian Church has to perform mental somersaults, it flips from a literal meaning to a spiritual meaning and then back to a literal meaning again; it was a neat trick then, but totally transparent today. The Christian Church cannot have it both ways; the interpretation of this event has to be either a literal or a spiritual one, and the literal interpretation has no clothes, the same as the literal Mary at the literal point of conception.

In the spiritual interpretation of this event, the conception and birth of Jesus takes place entirely within Mary's bodymind. According to Gnostics, the virgin label was only applied to indicate this was not a conception that took place in the normal physical way, but in a spiritual way. Mary was portrayed as a physical virgin although this does not have to be the case for the process to take place. In this version of events, Jesus is conceived by the Virgin Mary in her spiritual womb, the water centre, corresponding in a woman with the physical womb, after Joseph, Mary's male spirit, had spiritual intercourse with Mary's own female soul. Jesus is conceived spiritually in Mary's spiritual womb and grows to full term. The baby Jesus is conceived in a place where animals are fed, the tamed Horse of God. He is delivered through the eye of the needle, the spiritual birth canal, to take his place in the Kingdom of God, above the diaphragm, into the heart of Mary. Mary has embraced the masculine side of her nature and becomes one within herself, spirit and soul united as one. In this analogy Jesus represents the Christ, which is the spiritual entity that has been created. This is the reason why Mary is so important to Gnostics, *she* is the Divine One.

Other Gnostics expanded on the story of Jesus as an adult. In these analogies, the story of Jesus takes place within his own bodymind, and the apostles are just different facets of his own personality. In the gospel of Thomas (NHL 32.10-11 118), Jesus' ego is portrayed by his twin brother Thomas, who is always criticising and doubting Jesus' ability, hence Doubting Thomas. Also in the Gospel of Thomas, Judas Thomas is also portrayed as Jesus' twin brother, they are one and the same, a symbol of Jesus' ego. In this spiritual account, Judas is the real hero of the last supper. It is

Judas who ensured that Jesus went through with the spiritual process when Jesus was having personal doubts, and wanted God to take the cup, the Holy Grail, from his lips. Judas laid down his life so that his best friend should live; the clue is in Judas being found hanging upside down, a reference to the spiritual process in which light is reversed, and is an indication to reverse the meaning; and the thirty pieces of silver? Silver is another important symbol for reflection and is another reference to the reflective process. Whether one believes the spirit exists or not, even an atheist would have to agree, that a spiritual interpretation of Jesus' life makes more logical sense than a literal interpretation and is much more consistent.

Now that we know what the secret is and the secret code with which Gnostics hid the secret in their gospels, we can look back in hindsight and see the true meaning of some of the stories and obscure parables in the Bible, which now with the new interpretation and 'new eyes', make perfect sense. There was no literal crucifixion of Jesus, the physical Jesus did not die on the cross, but the real spiritual Jesus did. Crucifixion certainly took place in Jesus' day and Gnostics saw the potential of superimposing the spiritual process onto it. Jesus on the cross is symbolic of the suffering experienced as the ego dies, and the cross is symbolic of the pentacle, the bodymind. Rosicrucians still use the cross as the symbol for their spiritual process, the rose being symbolic of the emotional centre opening up at the heart. The spear, the Spear of Destiny, that the Roman centurion Longinus used to make sure that Jesus was dead, is symbolic of the inner reflected light thrust through point A in the bodymind, passing through the eye of the needle to puncture Jesus' heart at point B in the bodymind causing royal and holy blood to flow into the Holy Grail, within Jesus' chest. Jesus dying on the cross is symbolic of the achievement of the Holy Grail. All of this taking place on a spiritual level.

The practice of baptism is symbolic of the purification process, cleansing the bodymind with the inner light acting as water. Jesus did not literally walk on water; he symbolically walked on spiritual water, the inner light. Keeping the spiritual circulation flowing is known in Gnostic terms as 'walking on water'. John the Baptist spoke of one who was to come after him, he was also a symbol of the ego that died so that Jesus should live and John's head cut off and presented on a silver platter was confirmation of that. The severed head is symbolic of the dead ego killed by the reflected light indicated by the *silver* platter. Templars were accused by their inquisitors of worshipping a severed head, which they could not deny, but what they were actually worshipping was only symbolic of the death of the ego.

In other stories, Jesus turned water into wine, which is symbolic of the inner light being transformed into royal and holy blood. Wine is symbolic of royal and holy blood produced by the secret process, a process that requires matured grapes on the vine, those blue apples in parchment four, the grapes are the Chakras, the bodymind is the vine, hence the opposite description of withered grapes on the vine, which Jesus used quite often to describe the spiritually dead. He was referring to all of us whose Chakras have not developed and remain withered like those grapes on the vine. Jesus struck a stone with a stick and made water flow from it; a stick, staff or spear represents the inner light, and the stone is also a term used by Gnostics for Chakras, and the water that flows is the circulation of the light which is converted to royal and holy blood. The last supper, when the apostles ate bread and drank wine as symbolic of Jesus' body and blood, was bread of heaven and royal and holy blood that nourished them spiritually. Each of the apostles in this analogy are now individuals in their own right and undergoing the spiritual process which Jesus symbolises, each of the apostles becoming a Christ.

The 'burning bush' that both Moses and Saul encountered, is the tree that burns without being consumed, the Sephiroth, the Tree of Life that one has to ignite within oneself to reach the Kingdom of God and which may be the origin of the Christmas tree which traditionally accompanies the spiritual birth of Jesus. 'To hide ones' light under a bushel' is a direct reference to the spiritual process, in which one has to ignite ones' light source spiritually from the centre of ones' being, by energising one's sun centre. Your own sun is the light source that illuminates your entire spiritual body, and the bushel refers to your diaphragm, the upturned bowl or lid that prevents that light shining. "The lion shall lay down with the lamb", refers to the heart and head becoming one; the lion, Leo, symbol for the heart, and the lamb, a *new-born* ram, symbol for Aries the head, lamb of God.

The story of Mary Magdalene washing Jesus' feet is symbolic of the purification process. Mary is actually Jesus' own spirit, the female aspect of his nature who washes his feet with the inner light, just as in the secret process, and afterwards, on reflection, they enjoy spiritual intercourse, and create one new-born spiritual entity, a Christ. This is the reason Mary was closer to Jesus than all the other apostles. And the problem of the three Marys? There is no problem for a Gnostic. The three Marys symbolise the three aspects of the feminine; mother, lover and whore. They are one and the same, three aspects of the same entity, Mary.

What finally convinced me that Jesus was not a real person is, if he had been a real person, he would have been more helpful to us; he would have been more specific about how we were to follow his lead and be like him in order to reach the Kingdom of God. But he does not do that. Jesus talks to us in obscure parables and stories, in which he begins to sound just like a Gnostic scribe, revealing everything to us, but the secret itself.

In the end it should not matter whether Jesus was a real person or not, what really matters is what he stood for and remains a beacon for: truth, justice, courage, love, moral values principles and ideals, kindness, compassion, concern for the poor and oppressed, a belief in the reality of God, and the promise of an everlasting life in the Kingdom of God after death. This is what Gnostics' stories were written for, to inspire us to these ideals, these higher aspirations. What does it matter if Jesus lived or not, we still have his principles to live by; and yet to most Christians, it is crucial that Jesus lived, that he died on the cross, was buried and resurrected after three days. To accept that all these things really happened, exactly as it was written in the Bible, requires an absolute belief in the literal interpretation of events, because once one accepts Jesus as a real person, then one is literally committed to go down that route of an absolute literal understanding, from which it is so difficult to return. Why is it so crucial to your belief that Jesus lived?

The Jesus that the Orthodox Church has created has become a physical object that we worship as an icon, whilst failing to worship what he stood for. We worship the symbol of Jesus on the cross instead of worshipping what Jesus symbolises. Ironically, the Church has great difficulty in understanding spiritual concepts; there is a tendency to turn the spiritual concept into a physical object, and then mistake the object itself for the focus of worship. The Christian Church has turned matters of the spirit into laws, and then follows the letter of the law instead of the spirit of the law, and that letter of the law has led so many people astray that they have drifted far from the spirit of the law. I am with William Blake on this, with this excerpt taken from 'The Everlasting Gospel':

- The vision of Christ that thou dost see
- Is my vision's deepest enemy ...
- Thine is the friend of all mankind,
- Mine speaks in parables to the blind;
- Thine loves the same world that mine hates,
- Thy Heaven doors are my Hell gates, ...
- Both read the Bible day and night,
- But thou reads't black where I read white ...
- Seeing this false Christ, in fury and in passion,
- I made my Voice heard all over the nation.

In the eighth line Blake is imploring us not to take the Bible literally, to read between the lines not the written word itself, to read the spirit of the law and not the letter of the law.

Christians who take the Bible literally and believe that Jesus was a real person accept 'The Nicene Creed' as a statement of their faith. The Nicene Creed is a document based on the Creed of Nicaea which was produced at the 1st council of Nicaea in AD 325, under the direction of Constantine, a reworking of the earlier Apostles' Creed. The Creed of Nicaea was revised and finalised at the Council of Constantinople in AD 381. There are now so many different versions of the original Creed of Nicaea that it is hard to decide which one to choose to criticise, however, all of them agree on fundamental points so I have chosen the generally accepted Nicene-Constantinople creed, which is the creed that Catholics recite at Mass (Appendix 1). All of these are documents that Gnostics cannot accept, and which eventually led to their exclusion from the Christian Church. Gnostics do not have too much trouble with the first part of the creed, apart from the notion of 'God, the Father, ... '; God has no gender. They would take issue with 'the only Son of God', knowing that all Gnostics in a sense are begotten children of God. They could even accept Jesus Christ as 'of one being with the Father', as in being of the same essence as God, as long as this refers to the *infant* Jesus who existed only within Mary's bodymind as pure spirit. 'Was made man' infers that Jesus was somehow special, God in human form, whereas to Gnostics Jesus was just an ordinary man. These are just minor quibbles that Gnostic belief can accommodate at a stretch. However, towards the end of the creed it can be seen how the letter of the law begins to drift too far from the spiritual truth for Gnostics to accept. Notwithstanding the possibility that Jesus was not a real person, nevertheless Gnostics accepted, had he lived, he may have gone through all those experiences of suffering, had he been crucified, after all, they wrote the story to be symbolic of that process. But what Gnostics can never accept is that Jesus the *man* was 'of one being with the Father', as in the same essence as the Father. An atheist can accept that statement because they would argue they both only exist as imaginary concepts, but what is not possible for a Gnostic to accept is the belief that Jesus ascended to heaven with the same body, a physical body, and he is to come again with the same physical body. Gnostics as rational people knew that this was just not physically possible, and that their stories had been taken all too literally. Gnostics saw that the council of Nicaea, had not only confused a spiritual understanding with a literal understanding, but had also confused Jesus the infant in the first part of the creed with Jesus the man in the rest of the creed. These four elements, two separate issues, have been conflated to produce one flawed document in an attempt to explain everything to everyone's satisfaction. Spiritual truth did not appear to be on the agenda at Nicaea or Constantinople; but the major error occurs halfway through the creed: "For us and for our salvation he came down from heaven ... For our sake he was crucified under Pontius Pilate, he suffered death and was buried." It is just one inconspicuous little word, appearing three times and containing just three letters, three letters of the law. But this error in interpretation rests on the definition of that small insignificant little word that has had catastrophic consequences for humanity. The word is *'for'*, and the disastrously damaging phrases are *'for us'*, *'for our salvation'*, and *'for our sake'*. The misunderstanding has occurred over the interpretation of what the word 'for' means in this context. Orthodox Christians believe in the literal meaning of the word 'for', as in 'Jesus died *for* us', he died to save us, and because he did it *for* us, we do not have to do anything, he died for us and because of that we are all saved, we just have to believe in Jesus and we will all go to heaven and live a life everlasting. This definition of the word *for* is 'in place of', or 'to the advantage of', but the Gnostic spiritual meaning of the word *for* in this context, is 'to show us the way', *'for us to see'*, 'so we can observe', so that we know what to do and how to follow. Jesus died 'for' us in this sense of the word only. We see that message all the time on billboards outside churches and its derivatives, 'Jesus saves', 'Believe in Jesus and be saved', 'Jesus died for our sins', 'Jesus died to save us from our sins', 'Jesus died that you may live'. Having just typed that out, I suddenly realise that last one is actually true, but only true in a spiritual sense, the others are all false whichever way you look at them. The enormous consequences of that misunderstanding based on a literal interpretation of those phrases has meant that millions, probably billions of people have gone to their graves believing they were saved, when they were not, and thousands more continue to do so each day.

Gnostics know that we have to achieve our own salvation in this life by our own efforts in order to reach the Kingdom of God. Jesus saved himself and by doing so showed us the way. Jesus raised people from the dead, but not literally; he showed how we can raise ourselves from being spiritually dead. He raised himself from being spiritually dead and became spiritually alive. Jesus did not and will not raise the physically dead from their graves, rational people know that it is impossible. We are all spiritually dead, like those grapes withered on the vine, unable to produce wine because our Chakras remain undeveloped. We have to achieve our own resurrection here on earth in this lifetime by baptising ourselves with the holy liquid, the royal and holy blood. That is what we should all be striving to achieve at all times, this is the meaning of life. Did we really think that we could just say we believe in Jesus and then be saved and live forever? It was never ever going to be that simple. "If you bring forth what is within you, what you bring forth will save you. If you do not bring forth what is within you, what you do not bring forth will destroy you," (Gospel of Thomas, 45.29-33 in NHL). What is within you that's slowly destroying you is your ego, and what is within you that will save you is your soul.

It is a wonderful thing hindsight; one can look back at events and understand what probably happened and why. With the inner light shining like a torch it is possible to look back at that dark period when the gospels were first set in stone and became the letter of the law. We will never know for sure who the first Gnostic was, some say it was Hermes, but there can be no doubt now that Gnostics were the very first holy people, based on their personal knowledge of God. There is only one God, there is only one way to know God, and that is the way that Gnostics discovered many thousands of years ago, there is no other way to know God. This is the way that Gnostics have tried to teach the world, and that way is the secret meditation technique or prayer revealed in Poussin and Teniers' paintings. Some time someone somewhere gained access to God through this method. They did not call themselves Gnostic then, we have only come to describe that experience as Gnostic in the recent past, but it is the same experience, as it was for Gnostics of the past, as it is for Gnostics of the present and will be for Gnostics of the future. There is only one true experience of God and that is a Gnostic experience. Any future student of Gnosticism would do well to start from the premise that the Gnostic experience of God is at the root of all true religions of the past, the present and the future.

Gnosticism was never going to become a mass religion. It took years of self-denial, self-sacrifice and self-discovery to become a Gnostic. This was never going to catch on fast. One could not just call oneself a Gnostic and then become one, but a religion in which one only had to believe in Jesus to be saved from one's sins was certainly going to become popular very quickly. No years of hardship or self-knowledge required here, and what's more one only had to say one was a Christian to become one. So as Christianity grew in popularity, Gnosticism was pushed to one side to become a mystic branch of Christianity within the Church itself, a kind of existential philosophy on which all religions are based.

Over time the literal interpretation of the gospels predominated over the spiritual interpretation. A literal meaning or a spiritual meaning of the gospels became the dividing issue between Orthodox Christians and Gnostic Christians and there was no common ground between the two. There can be no co-existing literal and spiritual truth, one excludes the other. There can be two co-existing literal and spiritual meanings as we have already seen. The two meanings can happily co-exist as long as the literal meaning eventually leads to the spiritual truth. But when the literal meaning supersedes the spiritual truth and leads billions of people astray, then a grave error has occurred. With the key to the secret process we now know what Gnostics know, that Jesus was probably not a real person, he was just a man in a story made up to highlight a spiritual process. There is also only one way to interpret the gospels and that is in spiritual terms. A wholly literal interpretation of the Bible is wholly wrong. The literal meaning in the Bible and gospels are to be used as a reference to guide one to spiritual truth, and not to be taken as the truth itself. Gnostics have always been pointing to God, but we have only ever been worshipping their finger.

The issue of a literal or a spiritual interpretation of biblical events becomes entwined with the power struggle that inevitably took place within the Christian Church after Jesus' death. The individuals who rose to positions of authority within the Christian Church were ambitious individuals who sought positions of power, privilege and status whereas Gnostics avoid positions of authority, believing all are equal before God. So it was always likely to be those individuals who were not Gnostics and who believed in the literal truth of the Bible who would eventually rise to power in the Church. The Christian Church and its leaders, the bishops, priests and deacons, those who believed in the literal interpretation of biblical events, would be the ones who later came to decide which gospels would be rejected, and which gospels would accommodate their beliefs and be included in the final version of the Bible. For an excellent analysis of the power struggle that took place in the early Christian Church and how the structure of that Church we see today came about read 'One God, one bishop', in *The Gnostic Gospels* (E. Pagels, 1979).

I am more interested in why the power struggle occurred in the first place, even allowing for the fact that power struggles are an inevitable part of any organisation with a hierarchy. Had those early Christian leaders, such as Tertullian, Iraneus, Clement and Ignatious, been able to conceive of the spiritual truth in the gospels, then a power struggle would have been less likely, because they would have recognised early Christian Gnostics, such as Valentinus and Arius' greater wisdom. It is a mystery why Tertullian and others were blind to the spiritual truth, because they set the pattern, not only for subsequent Church leaders and the laity alike, but also for the way the Christian Church developed into what we see today. This issue is at the heart of what Jesus was referring to when he described people as having eyes but unable to see and ears but unable to hear. He was talking about seeing and hearing spiritually. What is the mechanism by which we deny spiritual truth, by which we turn a blind eye and a deaf ear? Is it that we cannot see, that we do not want to see, or that it suits our purpose not to see? Can ignorance of the secret process alone account for the inability to comprehend a spiritual meaning? Certainly this would be a major factor, but not enough to account for the eventual dominance of Orthodox Christian leaders. One can be ignorant of the full facts, and yet still seek the truth, or more information from those who appear to know, as in deference to a higher knowledge and wisdom. There is a lack of deference by Tertullian and others towards Gnostics, perhaps born of *blind* ambition, and a disbelief in the possibility of having a direct experience of God. Faced with this possibility, Tertullian and the others have not asked the question, how? In their ignorance and irreverence, they have dismissed the possibility as a flight of fancy, skulduggery or trickery, and mocked the mere notion of it. This seems to be a recognisable feature of the ego, to doubt, ridicule, reject, deny and ignore anything that it cannot understand or that challenges its authority, but to do so intentionally without any attempt to comprehend, is an act of wilful ignorance and doubting scorn and betrays an underlying pessimism.

Those early Christian leaders were not evil men, they were just ordinary people who happened to believe in the literal meaning of the gospels because they firmly believed it to be the truth, and they thought they were acting in the best interests of the laity. Constantine, on the other hand, was a Roman Emperor, who saw an opportunity within the structure of the Christian Church to control the population, and did whatever was expedient to his political ends. Neither has the Christian Church been lying to us for all these years, one cannot lie unless one knows the truth. The Church has been ignorant of the full facts and has consequently misled billions of people. It is a tragedy of epic proportions and it is devastating to realise that many good men and women, who spread the news of Jesus in good faith and with good intentions, were actually leading people away from God. And that is the real irony, the Christian Church, and religion generally, rather than facilitating spiritual growth, has actually become a barrier between humanity and God. Each of us should strive to have an individual relationship with God, and the Church hierarchy has always got in the way of that. But the cruellest irony is that the more one believes Jesus was a real person who came down to Earth to save us all, the less likely one is to be saved. Paradoxically, atheists are nearer to the Kingdom of God than Christian churchgoers and believers, because humanists pursue those same eternal values that Jesus did. Unwittingly, they follow what Jesus symbolises and not Jesus the symbol. It is even more ironic that humanists in pursuing those values are painted by the ego as the agents of Beelzebub, trying to destroy society and the Church and everything it stands for. Ironically, they could be right, but for the wrong reasons.

So, is it wilful ignorance and the lack of any desire to learn about the secret process that is the reason why Tertullian remains blind? Not entirely, there is something else that determines this outcome. There is a pessimistic view of human nature and an elitism, revealed in Tertullian's attitude towards the idea of humanity sharing a personal relationship with God, perhaps based on a belief in original sin, in which case Tertullian may have felt that humanity was not worthy of having that sort of relationship with God and, only by introducing the priesthood as a more worthy intermediary, is any sort of relationship with God possible. Tertullian and the others also seem to want to believe in the magic, in the miracles, in the superstition, in the irrational, and the supernatural explanation of events in the Bible, rather than a logical and rational understanding. The reality of Jesus is magical enough in its own right, without having to introduce the supernatural. Perhaps in the end it all boils down to the fact that Tertullian and co. had no concept to understand the spiritual truth, they were unable to conceive of it as it was written in the gospels because they were limited by a pessimistic mind-set.

The model I have put forward in chapter 2 (Fig. 1.10) is the key and the concept for understanding the spiritual meaning in the gospels. The secret meditation technique and prayer shown in Poussin and Teniers' paintings is the concept that bridges the credibility gap, and allows us to see, to conceive of, the spiritual meaning that was intended by Gnostics. That is because this technique is the key that Gnostics used to write down the gospels and is therefore, the only key that will unlock their code of understanding and meaning. The Dead Sea Scrolls and the Nag Hammadi Library have both been around for over fifty years and yet Church academics and theologians appear locked in a collective torpor in trying to understand these re-discovered gospels. They appear to have no way of understanding the new information they now have and no context into which it will fit neatly. They appear at a loss with what to do with it. But the model I have put forward can place the new gospels into context, and the key to understanding them all is the secret meditation technique that Gnostics were describing in their gospels.

The final irony is that the relationship that exists between the established Christian Church and Gnosticism exactly mirrors and reflects the relationship that exists between the ego head centred consciousness of the West, and the concept of the bodymind. The ego took control of the bodymind just like the bishops of the Christian Church took control of the Gnostic Christian faith. Gnosticism, the spirit and soul of Christianity, was cast out of the Christian Church, just as our spirit and soul have been cast out of our Garden of Eden, our bodymind, by our ego. In this scenario, there is hope for reconciliation. The authority of the Christian Church leaders is the ego that has to give way, to defer, and according to the model, it must willingly give up its existence for something better to come. Similarly, the Christian Church will not disappear, it will transform itself based on a new wisdom, but this time it should recognise what the real authority is, and embrace its fellow long-lost brothers and sisters. We do not need religion anymore, but we do need a truly spiritual Church, working together, head and heart, Orthodox and Gnostic, as one united whole we can truly transform people's lives for the better, just as it always should have been.

The story in the New Testament about Jesus' birth and death works on several different levels, depending on which Gnostic scribe is putting their particular slant on the story, or their original presentation. The final analogy brings it all together in a more understandable whole. John the Baptist and Judas Thomas have both been portrayed as Jesus' ego in different gospels, and their deaths, so that Jesus may live, correspond to stage one of the process. Jesus becomes the purified one, having undertaken stage two of the process, and is a symbol of your new compliant and compassionate ego that knows it has to die for you, and wants to die for you, so that you may live on. In stage three of the process, Jesus truly dies for you on the spiritual cross within you. The death of Jesus is also the attainment of the Holy Grail, confirmed by the spear of Longinus, the Spear of Destiny piercing Jesus' heart, so royal and holy blood fills the vessel in his chest, the Holy Grail.

Jesus may not have been a real physical person, but the real spiritual Jesus is alive and well and lives within us all, in that small abandoned child that waits patiently for your return. Jesus is the symbol for the potential within us, the potential to live on after physical death. Jesus is within that part of yourself that you disowned, rejected, denied, many years ago. Jesus is your twin, your child of God, the orphan of humanity.

Implications for Psychology, Psychotherapy and Mental Health

The implications of the secret knowledge for psychology is that a new theory of personality is suggested, one that will change our concept of psychology and its practical application. A new theory of personality to accommodate the new knowledge we now have. A new theory of personality that embraces the concept of one whole body consciousness, the bodymind, and rejects the isolated head consciousness on the grounds that it is limiting to the search for truth and the real determinants of human behaviour. A new theory that will encompass the spiritual and emotional development of the soul and which recognises the ego as an obstacle to this growth process. In this new theory, the ultimate aim of the human organism is based on personal growth as a spiritual and emotional process, and not a mental process.

The theory has to accept that the ego, everything we believe ourselves to be, our personality, our thoughts, our beliefs, our desire for possessions, all act as a barrier to this ultimate aim of the real self. Our false self, the ego, is a social construct, developed in order to protect us, like a hard shell, but now inhibits us and restricts us, like a hard shell, whilst our real self remains undeveloped and dormant. A new theory is needed, based on spiritual and emotional growth, where the head is a servant of the real self and not its master.

In Western society we have a very head centred and mechanistic view of the human organism. Freud, like others that followed him, believed and accepted that the whole of our consciousness, that is, our conscious and our unconscious life, takes place within the head, the brain. He described our consciousness as being like an iceberg, with the visible 10% above the water, being our conscious thoughts, and the 90% hidden below the water, being our unconscious thoughts. But there was a much better analogy available to him: the human body, which, had he seen the comparison, may have changed his entire theory. In this analogy, the head is the 10% conscious where our thinking takes place, and the 90%, the rest of the body, is where our unconscious exists. The suggestion is that our unconscious is contained in the body, not the head, and not as thoughts, but as emotions, feelings, desires, longings and all our hopes and our dreams. It seems so obvious now, but that is how powerful the head centred mind set is. As well as accepting the concept of a bodymind containing the unconscious, the new theory of personality would also accept that the unconscious operates through a vital circulatory system contained in the bodymind. This circulatory system allows the free flow of vitality, emotional and sexual energy, Freud's libido, in the East, Chi and Prana, around the whole body, and it is this circulatory system, providing vitality to the entire system, that keeps the human organism functioning healthily and optimally at all times. Conversely, it is when this health providing circulatory system is interrupted or overwhelmed, that illness in one form or another, physical or mental, occurs.

Eastern philosophy, and Yoga in particular, views the mind and body as one mentally, emotionally and spiritually functioning whole, in which the free flow of Prana or Chi is vital to mental and physical health. It is a highly sophisticated system that attempts to understand and explain human experience and behaviour in physical, mental, spiritual and emotional terms. The system contains advanced breathing techniques, muscle stretching and relaxation exercises, designed to keep open the vital energy channels allowing the free flow of vitality, and the Chakra system is the theoretical model on which it is based. The whole system was designed and has evolved to maintain physical, spiritual, emotional and mental health within the individual based on the notion of harmony between head and body. Should not the existence of such a system, have made psychology, psychotherapy and psychiatry in the West just a little bit curious? Incredibly, in all their history, none of them have ever embraced this holistic philosophy in any attempt to understand human behaviour or mental illness. In fact the British Psychological Society does the exact opposite; it frowns upon any alternative to its own philosophy, disapprovingly. It scoffs incredulously at the temerity of the mere suggestion that there could be any other way of analysing human behaviour. The attitude of the British Psychological Society to the holistic concept of the human organism reminds one of the Church's attitude towards Gnosticism, any criticism of the currently accepted dogma is regarded as blasphemy, and its critics, heretics. Is this just the lack of a concept again, which prevents them from conceiving new possibilities, or is it just the wilful ignorance of a closed mind? I can add a new adjective to the growing list, because it is this *arrogant*, wilful ignorance that is so difficult to understand. Faced with a system that claims to provide physical, spiritual, mental and emotional harmony, mainstream Psychological, Psychotherapeutic and Psychiatric Societies have not asked the question, "How is this possible?" They have not followed it up with any research into the validity of this claim, instead they have ignored it, denied it, rejected it and ridiculed it. Psychology and psychotherapy are the new religions of our age, with their laws set in stone; any attack on them is seen as heresy, but laws are made by man, they should be reviewed regularly, time changes everything, what was true of past generations is not true of this generation, paradoxically we have to change to remain the same, we have to update the letter of the law in order to retain the original search for truth and the spirit of the law.

Sigmund Freud came to the conclusion that repression of one's sexual energy was the root cause of the types of behaviour he observed in his clinic. We are to accept that this sexual energy is repressed by the unconscious mind with defence mechanisms, e.g. projection and sublimation. In his theory, Freud does not explain how the defence mechanism is created, Freud leaves us to work out ourselves what the mechanism is that creates the defence mechanism. Is it unconscious mental activity that creates them? If so, then the theory presents us with a fait accompli, because a defence mechanism is a particular behaviour not a mechanism that brings about the behaviour. The argument is tautological; the defence mechanism has become both the mechanism and the behaviour simultaneously, but without acknowledging how the mechanism creates the behaviour. We are expected to accept that these are unconscious mental processes, which we are not aware of, that prove that unconscious mental processes exist. The argument is circular, it is a neat trick, but which leaves an intellectual vacuum, and we are left to assume that this is what must happen, because there is no alternative.

But there is an alternative theory that does have some intellectual integrity. Freud abandoned his original theory of 'toxic libido', in which he believed that sexual energy became poisonous to the human organism when prevented from following its natural course, and this toxicity caused the perverted sorts of behaviour and neuroses he observed. He should have persevered with it. One of Freud's own students, Wilhelm Reich, expanded on the toxic libido theory; he believed that the mechanism that repressed not only our sexual energy, our libido, but also our emotional energy and our vitality, was muscular tensions within the body. The ego learns to control any uncomfortable or highly charged emotions and feelings by contracting its musculature against those feelings, preventing them from flowing freely and being experienced as emotional pain. The chief weapon in the ego's armoury is the diaphragm, a major muscle in governing the breath cycle. By controlling and restricting the diaphragm, the ego not only represses the breathing and thus reduces the amount of energy in the system, but also prevents the free flow of emotional energy from the lower body to the upper body. The ego learns to control our emotions by armouring itself against them in fixed, rigid muscular holding patterns, which reveal themselves in a physical body language, the way we hold ourselves. Over time this pattern of holding becomes fixed in our musculature, and becomes our normal way of responding, our character armour (Reich, 1972). Holding back bad feelings or painful memories may appear to be beneficial for the individual in the short term, however, this approach by the ego over the long term is self-defeating because the same muscular tensions that hold back the bad feelings also repress the good, natural health giving and healing emotional vitality that is necessary for a healthy functioning body and mind. A particular type of massage aimed at specific groups of muscles, was one of Reich's techniques for overcoming muscular tensions and returning the free flow of sexual and emotional vitality (Reich's orgone), in conjunction with the full breath cycle, and at the same time fully experiencing the repressed emotion. Reich was also one of the first to realise that the therapist had to engage with the client's negative transference first, if any progress was to be made.

The new psychology and psychotherapy would need to embrace a theory of personality in which the free flow of health giving vitality is paramount, and it is the ego that prevents this with the use of muscular tensions. It would also accept that the body contains our unconscious mind in the form of our feelings, our emotions, our hopes, our dreams and our desires; our unconscious life is the experience of all of these feelings. Muscular tensions in the body and our breathing is the mechanism by which our feelings, our emotions, our sexual energy and our vitality become repressed. Freud's defence mechanisms are thus the result of repressed emotions and not the repressing agent itself. The repressed feelings that enter our awareness are converted to thoughts and it is in the process of conversion that the defence mechanisms are activated, usually projection, in order to protect one's opinion of oneself. A psychology and psychotherapy already exist that encompass all these values, in Yoga. This discipline embraces many different techniques for improving the optimal functioning of the individual, e.g. stretching postures, breathing, relaxation, meditation, but one of the main objectives of Yoga, and also Buddhism, is to rid oneself of one's desire. The only difference between Yoga and the psychological and psychotherapeutic system I am proposing is in how to rid oneself of desire. In my proposal I am suggesting that this is achieved by destroying the thing that creates desire, and that is an avaricious ego. The only way of destroying the ego is by the secret meditation technique revealed in Poussin and Teniers' paintings.

And so the final factor the new theory of personality has to embrace is that the ego is the barrier to personal growth. It is the ego that keeps us locked into futile and dysfunctional ways of behaving. The negative transference that Reich found to be the main problem in the way of change was the ego defending itself. Reich did not realise it is the ego that has to be removed, to effect change, and not just be persuaded to co-operate. The ego will tell the therapist anything they want to hear as long as it does not have to change, change is something the ego does not do willingly. Present day psychotherapy can never effect change in the client's behaviour, because it does not address the real problem, the problem of the ego that does not want to change. Any psychotherapy that wants to effect any real change needs to tackle the ego first and persuade it that it needs to make way for something better to come. The only way of overcoming the power of the ego is the method shown in Poussin and Teniers' paintings.

If this theory is correct and the only way of effecting real change is by destroying the ego then it follows that all psychotherapy in the past and the present is doomed to failure, and is a waste of time, money, energy and resources. Yet a whole industry has built up based on Freud's Psychodynamic Therapy. Empire building psychotherapists have developed very rewarding careers based on a therapy that has no real validation. Psychodynamic Therapy has become like a religion, with any criticism of it being treated as blasphemy, but it has continued because nobody can dispute what they say or see any alternative. But a little urchin can see that Psychodynamic Therapy has no clothes, and armed with the key to change, the secret process, we have the alternative, and can see that Freud's theories are no longer appropriate for today's world because the ego is not mendable, it is expendable.

Freud was very pessimistic about human nature, and this is reflected in his psychological theories. To Freud, the unconscious is a seething cauldron of lust, a cesspit of perverted desires, a dustbin where the conscious mind dumps all the rubbish it cannot cope with, or does not want to deal with. But the psychological theory I am proposing is the exact opposite, in that the unconscious contains natural positive energy and is a literal treasure trove of inspiring ideas, of creativity, originality and artistic talent where pure genius is just plucked out of the ether. In its purest form the unconscious contains the notion of Ruskin's noble savage. This positive energy only becomes perverted when it is repressed by the ego and has to strive for an alternative outlet. In basic terms, Freud believed the unconscious was naturally bad, full of perverted sexual desires, and that it needed to be repressed by the ego in order to control those forces. I think we should look at it the other way round, the unconscious being naturally good and full of positive desires and emotions, which only become perverted *because* of repression by the ego. It is Freud's ego that is the problem, not the id. The ego represses the id, thus causing it to become a perverted savage beast, which the ego then uses as evidence to justify further repression. Now doesn't that sound familiar in a political context.

Psychiatrists are the experts on mental illness, they treat patients with medication in order to control their symptoms and behaviour and to ultimately effect a cure. Psychiatric theories of mental illness are based on the medical model, which is a very mechanistic way of viewing the human organism, and consequently sees mental illness as a physical malfunctioning of the brain. But as Szasz (1960) pointed out, if it is the brain malfunctioning, then why are these patients not sent to see a neurologist, who is a specialist that deals with brain disorders? Why do we have to create a whole new branch of medicine for this purpose? The answer is that mental illness has not always been seen as the result of a malfunctioning brain, that is just the prevailing idea at this moment in time. In more enlightened times more emphasis has been placed on mental illness being the result of problems of living. There are thus two competing ideas about the causes of mental illness, each one having a stronger or weaker influence depending on the particular ethos of the times. The medical model is a very head centred view of the human organism, reflecting the head centred philosophy of Western civilisation. Psychiatry, as all human sciences are, is incapable of conceiving of a whole body consciousness, a bodymind, or is this arrogant, wilful ignorance? Consequently any malfunction in behaviour has to be caused by a faulty brain. Whereas, if one looks at the human organism as one whole conscious system, the bodymind, then mental illness, the malfunctioning of the brain, is more likely to be caused by the repression or malfunctioning of the free flow of vitality around the bodymind system and perhaps especially to the head, where there is often a head and body split . If there is a malfunction in the brain, then this will have been caused by an imbalance in the bodymind due to an interruption or a surge in the free flow of vitality, in which case medication cannot cure mental illness, because it has no effect on the real problem, which is blocked vital energy. Medication can only treat the physiological symptoms in the brain and the resulting behaviour, which is rather like papering over the cracks, the effect is cosmetic, and would explain the 'revolving door syndrome', which indicates that people who suffer from mental illness are never cured by medication because they return to hospital time and time again. What sort of a professional service is this, when an illness one expects to be treated and cured by experts in their field, turns out to be just a temporary reprieve? If one went to a general hospital with a broken leg, one would be entitled to feel a bit disgruntled, if the leg kept breaking again, you would at least ask for your money back, especially when you discover that treatment only included a sticking plaster. But mental health patients have to accept this ridiculous state of affairs because they are led to believe there is no alternative, and are informed very patronisingly that it is 'all part of their illness'. The malfunctioning brain is just a symptom of the problems of living in a malfunctioning society. Mental health exists when the bodymind is working in harmony, head and body, brain and heart. Mental illness indicates some form of blockage, repression or surge in the circulation of vitality around the bodymind. Medication just removes the need for the government to address the real cause of mental illness, the problems created by a malfunctioning society. The medical profession colludes unwittingly in maintaining a corrupt political system.

The most effective psychiatric treatment for severe depression, and as a last resort for all depression, is Electroconvulsive Therapy, the effectiveness of which is quite dramatic and life-saving in a number of cases. ECT involves passing an electric current through the patient's brain in order to induce a seizure. During the seizure the body contorts in muscular convulsions and spasms that can last for thirty seconds or even longer, in which the whole body shakes vigorously under extreme muscular tension, even though patients are routinely given muscle relaxing medication to help prevent serious damage to themselves. This therapy was not found through the normal channels of scientific discovery, based on a hypothesis followed by a series of double blind trials in order to validate its efficacy, but accidentally from the simple observation by nurses on the ward, who noticed that patients who were severely depressed and who subsequently went on to experience an epileptic fit, seemed to be less depressed after having had the fit. Consequently, psychiatry has no idea how or why ECT is effective at all. It is a highly embarrassing state of affairs for psychiatry when there exists a very effective psychiatric treatment, but no psychiatrist either knows or understands how or why it works. But I have a hypothesis and a theory about how and why ECT is so effective. There are two main physical events that occur during ECT. Firstly, and considered to be the treatment, an electric current is passed through the brain, and secondly, and considered to be the side effects of the treatment, the whole body goes into convulsion. So the answer to how and why ECT is effective can only be based on one of the two physical events or even both together. Is it because the brain has been shocked back into its normal functioning, a default setting? Or could it be that every muscle in the body has been sent into spasm, thus releasing all the tension within the muscles and allowing the normal flow of health giving vitality to resume. There was a 50/50 chance of getting it right, but psychiatry got it wrong by opting for the head centred brain and mechanistic explanation, which ironically has no mechanism. Faced with an effective treatment with no theoretical basis, psychiatry has not sought a theoretical model that might explain why the effects occur, they seem to have just thrown their hands up in the air in amazement and done nothing, except take the money and run. The real reason ECT works is the second option, but we are all blind to it because of our ego's head centred mind-set. It could even be argued that the anaesthetic and the muscle relaxant could aid or even hinder the release of muscular tensions, but since anti-depressant effects of a seizure were observed prior to the use of these drugs, then it has to be the muscular contractions that are the main effective treatment in ECT. Psychiatry does not know how or why ECT works, but it refuses to explore or even countenance any other possibility because they have no concept for any other possibilities. And yet the basis for this theory has been around for over one hundred years with Wilhelm Reich, and psychiatry has dismissed it, ignored it and ridiculed it. This is how powerful the rational ego head centred mind-set is, it makes us blind to any other possibilities. ECT is a very barbaric and expensive way of achieving the same end results as Yoga, by the release of muscular tension and the restoration of the natural flow of vital energy. In the most severe cases ECT would still be needed for its immediate life-saving properties in a patient who has stopped taking fluids, but for ordinary mild to moderate depression, Yoga would be much more beneficial for the patient and cheaper too, but also less stressful for the soul which has to undergo a mini-death experience under ECT as the breathing routinely stops and the patient has to be artificially respirated.

The National Health Service claims to have adopted a new holistic approach to mental health care and in this respect has made some progress over the past twenty years, but compared to Eastern models of holistic health, the NHS model is only really a humanistic model, since it limits the physical side of our human nature to just its bodily functions and ignores the fact that the body has a spiritual and an emotional life, the body being the 'temple of the soul'. The NHS has hijacked the word holism, but has left behind the concept.

The NHS answer to spiritual guidance is to direct one to the nearest church. It is high time the NHS grasped the full concept of holistic health care otherwise it will leave itself liable to be prosecuted under the Trades Description Act. The NHS needs to adopt a real holistic model of mental health care and not continue as at present, with a holistic model that just pays lip service to the idea. The new holistic model would be one that viewed the human organism as one whole conscious being, a bodymind, that strives for spiritual and emotional growth. We as individuals need to take full responsibility for our own spiritual growth and not rely on religious guidance from others. A mental health professional would act as a psychotherapeutic spiritual advisor based on the new theory of personality, a facilitator for spiritual and emotional growth.

Mental health does not need psychiatry anymore, we do not need a medical model to understand mental illness, because we do not have a brain centred consciousness, which is the basic premise on which that model is based. Human beings appear to be the only animals on the planet that exhibit symptoms of mental illness, except for those animals confined in cages or restricted by other means from carrying out their natural behaviour. Does that not tell us something about the world we have created for ourselves, and does it not also tell us something about the nature of mental illness? These animals did not show signs of mental illness before they were locked in cages or was it just bad luck that only the poorly ones were chosen? Environmental stress created by a malfunctioning society causes mental illness, not a faulty brain. Mental illness is not a disease, it is not a medical condition despite psychiatry and society's best attempts to medicalise the problem. These are not new ideas, they are the enlightened and progressive ideas from the 60s and 70s put forward by such people as R.D. Laing and Thomas Szasz (1960) and which are even more relevant today. Mental illness should not fall into the province of medicine; it is a social problem caused by living in a stressful society and as such should fall within the remit of the social services. Medication would still be needed in the short term to control symptoms and extreme behaviour, but not to effect a cure. This medication could be prescribed by and dispensed by mental health professionals, whilst simultaneously undergoing the new therapy until we can change the political system that causes the problems in the first place.

Political and Social Implications

A seven year old child had such a strong sense of justice that they thought, "how much more just must the grown up world be?" Sadly, seven was about as just as it got.

After two world wars Britain was going to build a country fit for heroes. We tend to forget that in 1945 the people of Britain rejected the great hero of the second World War, Winston Churchill, in favour of a Labour Government, in a landslide victory on a wave of popular Socialist idealism, optimism and a hope for a brighter future for their children. They truly believed Britain was going to become their New Jerusalem. The Labour Party under the Atlee Government introduced the Welfare State, the National Health Service, a comprehensive education system and council housing for all. They were inspired by the possibility of achieving an Arcadian dream, a New Jerusalem, our Albion; but something went wrong with the crusade and 'the sword went to sleep in the hand'. Britain's ability to finance the dream stalled because the funds dried up; we still owed a massive war debt to America. After that, the Socialist Utopia never quite got up and running, there always seemed to be some obstacle in the way of progress, mainly lack of money. But they were patient, confident in the knowledge that the Promised Land was just around the corner. But in the 70s, Dennis Healy had to borrow massively from the International Monetary Fund who, in return, imposed strict financial constraints on Britain. Then in the 80s Margaret Thatcher 'clawed' back all the gains they had made and then announced there was no such thing as society and fostered the notion that greed was good and the idea of the enemy within, apparently I was one. Socialists knew the utopian dream was over when Tony Blair got rid of Clause 4 from the Labour Party constitution and then invaded Iraq in our name, based on a trumped up document and an exaggerated threat.

We are the 'baby boomer generation' who had it all. Our parents sacrificed everything so that their children would have a better world to live in, but we took that world and abused it selfishly for our own ends, and in the process became the pretentious hypocrites we accused our parents of being. We consumed everything without a care for the future and have given nothing in return. We baby boomers have trampled on the hopes and dreams that our parents had for our futures, that they tried to build for us by making personal sacrifices. What sacrifices have we made for our children and for the next generations? Have we made the world a safer place for them to live in? We wrap our children in cotton wool and pay scant regard for the kind of world we have created. What provisions have we, the baby boomers, made for our children, for their education, for their employment, and for a better safer world? Our parents would turn in their graves if they could see their sacrifices, their hopes and dreams lying in tatters. We, the baby boomers, stand accused of selfish wilful neglect of our children's future, welfare and safety. If we get that far, history will look back at our selfish generation with contempt.

One does not have to be a socialist to recognise that the Labour Party is not a party of socialism any longer. This distinction disappeared with Clause 4. Now how did that happen? One moment there is a Utopian dream, and then fifty years later, it's having tea with Rupert Murdoch, in Number 10, via the back door, of course. Tony Blair wanted power at any price even if political principles had to be jettisoned along the way. It must be hard to stick to one's political principles if one is being offered the possibility of a knighthood to drop them. And yet what happened to the Labour Party is a perfect analogy for what happened within the Christian Church all those years ago. Both organisations started off with a philosophy, a set of ideals and sound humanitarian principles. For Christianity, these were Gnostic ideals, and in the Labour Party, Socialist ideals. Both sets of ideals over time became side-lined, because of status-hungry individuals who coveted power at any price. We know that Gnostics were excluded from the Church in the end, and the time will come when the few remaining Socialists will also be excluded from the Labour Party, for Clause 4, just substitute any Gnostic gospel.

Whether you agree that capitalism is the best means of economic and social organisation of society or not, you would have to accept that it does seem to have provided a better standard of living for some. You can argue that it has civilised us, put food on the table, clothed us, and provided everything we need at the lowest price. But your view would depend on your definition of a better lifestyle, and if better in terms of quantity, at what price to our quality of life? But whatever one thinks of capitalism, however efficient it is at providing consumer goods, it can hardly be described as a fair and just system. A system where 90% of the wealth of the country is owned by just 10% of the people is not a just and fair system, and the fact that the people who have the power to ensure that the system remains in place are the 10% who own 90% makes it doubly unfair and unjust. This ratio seems to be a constant of a capitalist economic system. We all see this and we know it is unfair, so do we just tolerate this system because the alternatives seem far worse, or are we all just masochists? And what of our real self, our soul? The soul strives for something other than possessions, perhaps for a political system that would allow it to flourish.

I am a Socialist, a left winger, one of the loony left, a do-gooder, a commie, a red under the bed, a Marxist, Trotskyist, wet fully paid up member of the politically correct brigade, the enemy within, and I am not emigrating to Russia or Cuba, so there! Neil Kinnock was a great orator and an articulate Welshman and I liked Michael Foot's duffel coat and Red Ken. My hero is Tony Benn, the finest Prime Minister this country never had, a man who gave up his peerage for his political principles, unlike some politicians who give up their political principles for a peerage. A man of great moral courage and political integrity and yet who was mocked mercilessly by the media because he stuck by those principles, and now he is no threat to them, the media warm to him. I mention all this because these are examples of how the ego mocks and ridicules, in its ignorance, anything that might bring about political change, which seems to be a particular British trait, to make fun of things we are frightened of, it somehow reduces the threat. But those who poke the most fun are those in positions of political power, opinion leaders and the media is their mouthpiece. Socialists have become ashamed of their political values, they dare not declare them, they act like they are carrying a deadly contagious disease, no-one will want to know you if they find out. The Labour Party have lost their way, they are so browbeaten by the media that the poor things don't even know what they stand for anymore. Socialists should be shouting their ideals from the rooftops, "I'm a do-gooder and proud of it, stuff you, Rupert Murdoch," but instead have allowed Socialism to become a dirty word aided and abetted by the right-wing of their own party who sought power at any price even if it meant betraying their own colleagues. Socialism has become a political philosophy that dares not speak its name and it is our children and humanity who pay the price.

We all know the type of political system we need, we do and we know we do, it is self-evident, but our ego denies it. We know it in our hearts, our soul yearns for it. The spirit of truth, justice, honesty and compassion cries out in rage and frustration at the world we have created. This spirit of Jesus was at the French Revolution, at the American Declaration of Independence, with the Chartists and the Suffragettes, during the abolition of slavery, at the Russian Revolution, with Ghandi, with the people of Britain and the Labour Party in 1945, with the American Civil Rights Movement, and with Martin Luther King. This spirit that has compassion and love for fellow human beings, that champions the poor and oppressed, that strives for justice and truth, that strives for higher values and higher human aspirations, and makes no distinction on the grounds of race, colour, class, sex, age and creed. These are the ideals that recur throughout history, the ego represses them, but they can never be destroyed or denied for ever. They are eternal values, absolute spiritual principles, which we all recognise in our hearts. In 1776 the United States of America wrote their 'Declaration of Independence', *"We hold these truths to be self-evident , that all men are created equal, that they are endowed by their Creator with certain unalienable Rights, that among these are Life, Liberty and the pursuit of Happiness"*, and they are self-evident, we all know they are and we all agree with them in principle. However, the problem arises in the detail and the application of these principles. The meaning of freedom and liberty depends on how it is defined. We know in our hearts how freedom was originally defined when it was written into the declaration, which is freedom from exploitation of others, as in slavery, or freedom and liberty to be ourselves and to pursue happiness. But the meaning that came to prevail is the Conservative and Republican definition, which is freedom for Capitalists to exploit whatever and whomever in the pursuit of profit, which I know to them probably means happiness, but which leads to the exact opposite of the original meaning for the rest of us. The definition of freedom is only one of several fundamental ideological differences between Socialists and Conservatives, between the Left and Right in politics.

Surely it is not beyond the wit of humanity to design a political system that we can all agree on based on those eternal and absolute values, carefully defined of course. To do this one needs to identify the obstacles to achieving that and the ideological mind-set that prevents agreement on such a system. Ideologies can be reduced to their fundamental values, it's straight forward, we can all work it out. When one reduces Conservative ideology to its fundamental values, one is left with the principles of selfish greed and a pessimistic view of human nature, and I do not think a Conservative would radically disagree with that statement. Reducing Socialist ideology to its fundamental values, one is left with the principles of selfless compassion for others and an optimistic view of human nature. Conservatives have a pessimistic view of human nature, they judge others by themselves, they tend to believe in the literal truth in the Bible, they believe in original sin, that people are naturally bad and need to be controlled, and society protected from their animal natures by the law of the land. Conservatives think that Socialists are very naïve in this respect, and that Socialism will never work because of human nature being what it is. Socialists also judge others by themselves, they have an optimistic view of human nature, they believe people are naturally good, and need to be freed from unjust laws and from oppression, which will allow individuals to flourish and develop to their full potential. Socialists would like to change the capitalist political system because it is oppressive to the human spirit and soul, and feel that Socialism will work, because of people's natural goodness and desire to help one another for the common good, and because of human nature being what it is. Socialists feel that Conservatives lack compassion and empathy for others less fortunate than themselves. Ironically, Conservatism under capitalism has prevailed, and Socialism never really got started in Britain; it was thwarted by people who were natural pessimists. Conservatives are the people Conservatives warn us about, for Humanitarians they are the real enemy within, the enemy of humanity.

Assuming that selfish greed and a pessimistic view of human nature are not human attributes to be encouraged, one has to ask how these unnatural traits may have developed. I would suggest that the existence of these traits shows a lack of something else, and that something else is compassion. These traits exist when there is a lack of compassion and empathy for others, and the mechanism that brings about lack of emotion of any kind is muscular tensions, as postulated by Reich, expanded on by Lowen and later Dychtwald and Elsworth Baker. The upper classes, the public school boy, the people who go on to run our country and become the political opinion leaders are all socialised in a particular way to run the country by the best privileged schools. For example, at a public boys' school one of the first things children have to learn is how to control their emotions. It is a peculiar British trait to have a stiff upper lip, we are noted for it and apparently proud of this ability. When one feels strong emotions of any kind it is revealed in the upper lip as a tremble or a quiver which indicates all loss of emotional control and the beginning of a break down into tears. A public schoolboy is taught quite harshly and abruptly that this is not the done-thing, "stop snivelling, boy", and that one should never show emotion in this way, it shows weakness and is thoroughly un-British. The child very quickly learns to control that quivering top lip by cutting off the emotion at source with muscular tension. Unfortunately, this leaves the top lip void of any emotional response at all and it becomes frozen as a 'stiff upper lip'. This is an extreme example of what is, in most cases, a general response of varying degrees depending on the severity of the effect, but examples of the stiff upper lip do actually exist, especially at a higher social level, e.g. the ex-Prime Minister Douglas Holme. The British stiff upper lip is an indication of a person who has no emotional responses at all, perfect for running the country.

In 50s' and 60s' Britain, girls and boys were treated differently in mixed sex schools. Boys were punished severely and held accountable for their every misdemeanour, whereas girls were usually let off without recrimination for the same act. Nobody questioned the gross injustice of this at the time because it was generally accepted that females were the weaker sex and should not be punished like the boys. Looking back now, this was not only the socialisation process in action, but also sexism in action, boys had to be punished to toughen them up for a man's world out there in the world of work, whilst girls were not supposed to enter this world being considered altogether too fragile and only capable of becoming housewives and bringing up children. It all seems very quaint now, but this was the norm then. Boys had the spirit and their individuality castrated at school so that they could seamlessly enter the workforce as compliant units of labour. Women wonder why men have no emotions; it's because they had them knocked out of them by a socialisation process that was preparing them for the 'dog eat dog' world of capitalism. Illich (1971) even went as far as to say that the principle aim of schooling was not to educate our children but to socialise them to fit into society as it exists, "School is the advertising agency which makes you believe that you need society as it is" (p 114) and "School has become the planned process which tools man for a planned world, the principal tool to trap man in man's trap" (p 111).

The implication is that political opinions and one's political point of view are formed by the repression of the natural flow of healthy emotions by the ego. The British conservative personality formed from the cradle by the way we socialise our children, the way we force them to repress their natural emotions at an early age in order for them to fit into society, which might explain why as a nation we appear so obsessed with potty training. As above so below, the capitalist political system creates, through our parents and schools, exactly the type of selfish greedy personality it requires to service its rapacious nature, in perpetuity. This is the mechanism by which we become blind to our emotions and feelings, blind to reality, blind to our soul, blind to our ego's deviousness and blind to the workings of capitalism. Humanity has to break out of the prison that the ego has made for us. We have to break free from the ego's vice like grip, these 'mind forged manacles', and become human again as we once were as a child. "Man is born free, and yet everywhere he is in chains" (Rousseau, 1762).

Surely in our hearts we all want the same thing, a political system based on those eternal human values we can all unite around for our children's sake, as long as we can agree beforehand on the definitions and the small print. We are intelligent people, we can design a new political system based on those values. It does not have to be Socialism if that is too much of a tarnished image for some people. We could even come up with something better, some principle that cannot be derided or abused. The Equality, Justice, Truth and Freedom from Exploitation Party, and it would only have to have one clause enshrined within its constitution: "Any person that wants power in the party should never be allowed to hold it." Or, how about 'OPTIMISM'? The argument against a new political system based on optimism about human nature is that it will fail because human nature is not like that and "you cannot change human nature". But that argument cannot be used anymore because we can change human nature now. We have the secret meditation technique that can make us all more compassionate and less selfish human beings with an optimistic view of human nature, a technique to free our souls. This technique is not just aimed at Tories, we have to recognise what the real enemy is.

World politics seem to be based on paranoia, which usually ends in total humiliation for those afflicted, e.g. the Suez and Bay of Pigs fiascos. The concept of the Domino Effect terrified the U.S.A. so much that they helped to overthrow the democratically elected Socialist government of Salvador Allende in Chile. The Domino Effect was a theory based on a paranoid belief that if one country 'fell' to Socialism in South America then one by one they would all topple, so much for America's belief in democracy. Then there is Game Theory, which seems to be a highly sophisticated grown up version of paper, scissors and stone, in which one has to work out what your enemy might do next and then act pre- emptively. In the case of selling arms to other countries or invading other countries for their oil, the theory is, "If we don't do it someone else will." This is also based on the paranoid fear of being outflanked by the competition, but where is the morality in this self-serving logic?

The reason given for the invasion of Iraq was the threat and indisputable evidence, outlined by Tony Blair before Parliament, that Iraq had weapons of mass destruction which could be activated in forty-five minutes, the inference being that they were aimed at this country. But there never were any weapons of mass destruction, so either Tony Blair was lying to Parliament or this was based on pure paranoia or something even more sinister, e.g. both the Bush and Blair administrations accepted very unreliable intelligence that supported the need for war in Iraq, and dismissed an extremely reliable intelligence source that ruled out any need for invasion. It appears obvious now in hindsight, that the decision to overthrow Saddam Hussein had already been taken, and both governments were cherry-picking the evidence to suit the case for war. Is this rational human behaviour or are these decisions based on paranoia or even greed? Some may even say that the forty-five minute warning was designed to create paranoia in order to get people on board. And all the while Bush and Blair delivered their rationale for war in serious, concerned and measured overtones, we now know they were both being economical with the truth, and yet thousands of British people who demonstrated against the war, knew in their hearts that this war was not justifiable, because from the intelligence they were presented with, it didn't add up, e.g. the dodgy dossier; and the irony in all this is that any attempt to challenge the motives of the government, and the official line, as some did at the time, and it is they who are accused of being "paranoid conspiracy theorists." We all assumed that our leaders were rational and intelligent human beings, but the ego does not stop to consider its actions, it does not learn from its mistakes; Blair still insists it was the right decision to take; so now the invasion of Iraq will go down in infamy as the biggest international political blunder and war crime this country has ever committed, and what a precedent to set; the invasion of a sovereign country, on a pretext.

The ego is so foolish that it manages to create the thing it most fears, e.g. Al Qaeda; just a wild guess here, but I think the existence of Al Qaeda might have something to do with the West's arrogant invasion of sovereign Arab countries for their land and oil, and in the process humiliating and assassinating their leaders. What would our reaction be if the roles were reversed? Do we really believe that Al Qaeda are evil and enjoy being terrorists just to annoy us? Their response to the West is more like a normal human reaction to a big bully. Again we react to and blame the problem we have created and ignore the cause, instead of addressing Al Qaeda's genuine grievances against us and trying to resolve them. But there is no limit to the ego's paranoia because it is blind to itself, e.g. when the Arab people revolt and it is in the West's interests then it is called the 'Arab Spring' and we support them, but if not in our interests they become Islamist terrorists. We are our own worst enemy, Al Qaeda is a hideous reflection of ourselves.

Time is running out, we already have fundamentalist Christians in the White House. You may believe our leaders are sane and well-balanced individuals, but political egos like George Bush and Dick Cheney believe in the literal truth of the Bible and that Armageddon will occur just as the Bible predicts. So convinced are fundamentalists that this will happen that given the opportunity they will bring it about, thus confirming the literal truth in the Bible in a self-fulfilling prophecy: and these people have their finger on the nuclear button. And what of Tony Blair's role in the Middle East, does he also believe in the literal truth of the Bible? We have already had Afghanistan, Egypt, Iraq, Libya and now Syria all of these not a million miles away from Armageddon and this madness is getting closer.

Implications for Education

The relationship between the ego and the soul is like a person with a multiple personality, where one personality does not know of the others' existence. Likewise the ego has no awareness of the soul's existence, it is blind to it, "there is no other god but me". And yet once the ego recognises the soul's existence it will learn to have nothing but admiration for it. This eternal love story probably formed the basis for Shakespeare's *Romeo and Juliet*. Since the recent release of the film *Anonymous* (2011), there has been some debate about who the real author of Shakespeare's plays is. Gnostics know that Shakespeare did not write the Shakespeare plays, they were written by a Gnostic, possibly several Gnostics. The highest accolade for a Gnostic is to produce a great work of art and then take no credit for it. This humble act shows the utmost virtue of complete humility, that only someone with total control of their ego can achieve.

There are several candidates for the author of Shakespeare's plays, but Shakespeare is not one of them. The film *Anonymous*, puts forward a good case for Edward De Vere, Lord Oxford, but there were other valid candidates around at that time, Christopher Marlowe, and Francis Bacon in particular being an interesting example. Francis Bacon is reputed to be one of the founders of the Rosicrucian movement, probably the first English Rosicrucian and as such the first grandmaster to the 33rd degree, and would have had access to all the knowledge necessary to write the plays, and leave his mark. There is a specific example of an acrostic signature in *The Tempest*, Act 1, Scene 2, when Miranda speaks to Prospero:

> **B**egun to tell what I am, but stopp'd
> **A**nd left me to a bootless inquisition,
> **Con**cluding 'stay: not yet'

Pure chance one would think unless one already knows that Bacon wrote The *Tempest*, then it is not chance at all.

In *Henry IV*, the name Francis appears thirty-three times on the same page, sometimes in the most bizarre ways and seemingly in order just to reach that figure. The number thirty-three refers to the thirty-three degrees one has to climb to become a grandmaster of secret organisations based on Gnosticism, e.g. Freemasonry, and that number is based on the number of vertebrae in the human spinal column which is symbolic of the ladder, Jacob's ladder, one has to climb to reach the higher Chakras and the Kingdom of God; thirty-three was Francis Bacon's number. There is a well-known drawing of Francis Bacon with a full head of Hair, but with the hair removed it becomes the bald William Shakespeare; the two drawings are identical except for the '*air*. For a more detailed and compelling discussion on the case for Francis Bacon being the real author of the Shakespeare plays read 'Bacon, Shakespeare, and the Rosicrucians', in *The Secret Teachings of All Ages*, by Manley P. Hall (1977). From this evidence it is clear that even Ben Jonson knew at the time that the real author of Shakespeare's plays was Francis Bacon. It may even be that several Gnostics collaborated on this grand project to show their skill and understanding of the great secret.

All they wanted from William Shakespeare was his name which shortened sounds like "Will shake spear", a reference again to the spinal column, of which any long staff, shepherd's crook, or spear is a symbol, e.g. the witches' broom, but especially the spear which flies through the air so is also a symbol for the breath. In this instance, the act of shaking the spear is referring to the act of awakening the spiritual process by the power of the 'will' and the use of the breath. The question remains, why would anyone go to such enormous lengths just to undermine Shakespeare if there wasn't an element of truth to it? What would be the point? Unless of course Gnostics, were trying to tell us something more than just about Shakespeare, something more than just about themselves, something about the nature of human nature, perhaps about the way we would worship Shakespeare as an icon and ignore the truth of which he wrote, perhaps about the way the ego in its ignorance worships the physical and literal and remains oblivious to the obvious spiritual and emotional meaning all of which would perhaps unravel on Shakespeare's demise. What does it matter if Shakespeare wrote the plays or not, it does not make them any the less for that and we still have them to enjoy and to fully comprehend.

Richard III was the last Plantagenet King of England. The name Plantagenet derives from Henry II's father, Geoffrey of Anjou's custom of wearing a sprig of the 'planta genista' in his headgear during battle. Now the 'planta genista' is the Latin name for the 'broom', a shrub which as we have seen is very much associated with the secret process and much beloved by witches for *cleaning* out their houses. The Plantagenets reigned over Gascony, South-West France for many years, so it is possible they would have come into contact with Gnostic philosophy at that time, from Cathars seeking asylum from over the border. Shakespeare depicted Richard as an evil Machiavellian 'hunchback', which is strangely at odds with contemporary accounts of him and there are suggestions that Shakespeare exaggerated Richard's defects for his Tudor audience, but which was not without guile. As we have seen, Gnostics often gave the outward impression of the opposite of the truth for the unknowing and the exaggeration of the hump is critical here. There is one well-known animal that has a pronounced hump and that is the camel so there is an oblique reference to the secret process here also; these are all nods and winks to a fellow Gnostic. Shakespeare was covertly referring to Richard as a person who had undertaken the secret process. It is also interesting that Shakespeare's Richard III was often catalogued as a tragedy and not a history. The inference is that Richard's defeat at Bosworth was a tragedy not only in human terms, but also in terms of the secret wisdom which died with him near to Stoke Golding and Dadlington in the year 1485 and one wonders the direction that humanity might have taken had the Tudors never come to power. How prescient that the secret wisdom has come to light, at exactly the same time that Richard III's remains are uncovered, in the City of Leicester in the year 2012. The Great Secret has finally come home with the exhumation of Richard III's bones.

A logical and rational understanding of the world makes no allowance for human emotions; they don't really count, they are superfluous, irrational, but this short sightedness is a major omission in academic terms. Ignoring the potential of our emotions, denying their importance, is like not using all the faculties available to us, e.g. swimming and only using our legs to move forward because we don't believe our arms are any use to us, in fact sometimes we insist we have no arms at all. The ego, capitalism and Academia downgrade the importance of emotions when they are the very things that make us most human. The ego has no consideration for human emotions, they are unnecessary, and just like psychology and economics, capitalism makes no allowance for feelings in its theories and equations. For capitalism, people are just convenient units of labour, machine like automatons in our responses, entirely predictable in our behaviour, just individual units of consumption. The ego and capitalism proceed as if emotions do not exist, the soul does not exist, they do not have to be taken into consideration in its calculations, they are irrational, but they underestimate the soul at their peril, they have a blind spot, an Achilles heel. The ego and capitalism deny our emotions at all levels of life, just ask yourself what it is that stops you from showing emotions in public? What stops you from discussing feelings with your mates? Emotions and feelings are the enormous 'elephant in the room'. You can perhaps now see how the ego limits us all by denying there is anything more important than itself, but the ego is not completely 'armless. The ego, capitalism, Religion, Psychology, Psychotherapy, Psychiatry, Politically, Economically, Academically all get it exactly wrong because they are all blind to our emotions and feelings and fail to acknowledge the enormous power and potential contained within them.

The ramifications of this new knowledge are endless and effect all avenues of our lives. In education and at the top universities students will continue to be misled because emotions and feelings do not even show up on the academic radar. Like the debate between evolution and creationism, does one continue to teach a brain centred consciousness if a body centred consciousness has more credence, and we don't teach an Earth centred Universe anymore? This new knowledge is revolutionary; it turns everything on its head and presages a new age in evolutionary development, a new sense of being in the world, a new Age of Enlightenment, a Spiritual Renaissance. This new knowledge shakes the corridors of power and rattles the cloisters of Oxford and Cambridge and foretells of a seismic shift in our comprehension of what it is to be human. It places human emotions and feelings on a much higher evolutionary level than mere thinking. Emotions and feelings, the basis for our sense of being, circulate throughout the bodymind, the centre of our very being located at the tip of the solar plexus the sun centre, point **B**. A sun centred consciousness as the centre of our sense of being in the world is every bit as revolutionary as a sun centred solar system was in the 16th century. As above so below, the solar system on a macro scale is reproduced on a micro scale within the human body. Our bodymind is a solar system on a micro scale, our very being reflects the solar system in which we evolved and into which we were born. People laugh at 'Uranus', but how do you think it got its name? People notice that God spelt backwards is dog, and for this reason the dog has always been used by Gnostics to symbolise the opposite of God, i.e. a restless, howling, barking animal; how appropriate then to name the furthest planet from the Sun, Pluto. And Earth is our heart with just the transposition of that letter 'h' again. Mars reversed 's Ram, Aries the head. Mercury nearest to the Sun is another name for Hermes, the winged messenger nearest to God. The secret is all around us, but we don't see it even when we see it.

There is a science of human behaviour, psychology, a study of human thought, philosophy, but there is no formal study of human emotions and feelings. Surely this is a huge oversight, a serious blind spot in the Human Sciences and academic terms. "In the last century there was a neuroscience of emotions and today there is a neuroscience of the emotions. In between there was a long dark gap during which neuroscientists regarded emotions as elusive, objectively difficult to define, and thus not acceptable to study" (Antonio R. Damasio, 2005). This has also been true of all the human sciences, emotions and feelings were considered elusive and difficult to define (perhaps Damasio was diplomatically meaning irrational), so scientists in the past have worked around them or worse just plain pretended they did not exist. At least neuroscientists have now picked up that neglected gauntlet. One would expect the study of emotions and feelings to be the province of psychology, but the definition of philosophy, "the rational investigation of *being* and knowledge", puts it squarely in their court. However, philosophy has mainly concerned itself with systems of thought and never fully addressed the experience of our emotions and ironically of being, they have been playing mind games instead of seeing the elephant in the room. Philosophy as a discipline attempts to embrace both thinking and being simultaneously, but surely this concept is an oxymoron, thinking automatically excludes a sense of being, just as, if one wants to experience a sense of being one has to stop thinking. Try it for yourself, you don't need experts to tell you. You should find that whilst you are trying to think you lose any sense of being and conversely to attain a sense of being one has to suspend one's thinking processes. It is our ego thinking that prevents us from experiencing the experience of being human and of 'being'. It's time to stop thinking and start 'being' human again. "Close your eyes Luke, and feel the force." Paradoxically, we have to close our eyes in order to be able to see again, to learn to see with our entire being.

So let's get this straight, there exists a huge area of human experience, and some may say an area that most defines us as human beings, but here in the West there has never been any formal academic study of it, there is no formal science of the emotions, of feelings and consequently, of being. No concept exists to describe this subject, even though in the East a highly sophisticated system has existed for thousands of years. Here in the West emotions and feelings are considered irrational and therefore, not worthy of study. This is such an enormous oversight by the Human Sciences that I have to keep reminding myself that our emotions and feelings are what make us most human, unless of course even that is a matter of opinion. Is it the intellect of the brain or compassion of the heart? It depends on how one defines what it is to be human and listening to the experts it appears to be our intelligence and the ability to reason coupled with the use of language that defines us. So there you go then, your love counts for nothing. But hold on a minute, anyone would think these experts were talking about an alien species. I don't need an expert to tell me what it is to be human, I am human and I can experience it for myself and make my own mind up and in my experience I am more than just my intellect, my ability to reason and my ability to communicate. When I consider what makes me most human it is my feelings and a sense of 'being' in the world that is distinct from my intellect and my thinking, in fact thinking and reasoning actually prevent this sense of being.

I watched a TV programme recently about what makes us human in which the entire series was devoted to how extraordinarily brilliant our brain is, no mention of emotions or feelings at all. Is this blindness pandemic or is it just me that's wrong? It would be much easier for everyone if I were the one who was mistaken then nothing would have to change at all, so if they come to take me away, you will know why. For me the definition of what it is that makes us most human would always have to include the emotions of love, compassion and empathy as the most important criteria, with intellect, thinking and language way down the list. The alternative is a super intelligent, rational, articulate person who is as cold as a fish, hardly human at all. The question of head or heart is similar to the difference between intelligence and wisdom, e.g. intelligence is the tool with which we build wisdom, we use our brains to make sense of the world in order to anticipate future events, and learn from it. Once we have built our house we should put our tools aside, but we have ended up worshipping the tools instead of building anything; or like attempting a jigsaw and then only admiring the individual pieces instead of building the whole picture, of an elephant in a room. The new knowledge challenges the existing superiority of the intellect of the head theory, the centre of our thinking, and suggests the passion, will and wisdom of the heart not only defines us as being most human, but also locates point **B** in the bodymind, the tip of the solar plexus, as the centre of our sense of being, the centre of our consciousness and wisdom. You decide, are all the greatest philosophers in history mistaken? Are the top thinkers from the elite universities all wrong? Or is it just this little urchin that's misguided? The correct answer is, of course, all the greatest philosophers, all the top professors, all the great minds from the past and the present, and the reason they have no clothes is because they have not used all of the material available to them. They are not just armless, they are also eyeless, it is a dual denial, they are all blind to emotions and feelings within themselves and consequently blind to emotions and feelings in attempting to understand the world in which we live, they are blind to the wisdom and understanding accessible to all of us through our emotions and feelings. The new knowledge undermines everything you have ever believed to be true, are you ready for that new experience? Are you ready to open yourself up to new ways of learning, new ways of understanding, from the heart not the head? The excitement of the challenge is there for us all, open your heart to Gnostic wisdom.

You will not find Wilhelm Reich's theory of personality being taught in any establishment schools or universities because it is considered to be a heresy in academic circles, an idea to be mocked and ridiculed, but the new knowledge indicates that Reich's theory was nearer the truth than current theories will ever be. Reich's theory of personality was an idea before its time, a psychological theory that eventually dare not speak its name; even his books were burned. The tragedy is that Reich was driven insane by society and his peers' rejection and mockery of him, eventually to become a figure of fun, lampooned for all to see, to be incarcerated in a federal prison where he eventually died. Reich is the Van Gogh of psychology, the world was not ready to understand then, "they did not listen, they did not know how, perhaps they'll listen now". Reich's theory of personality should be retrieved from the dustbin of history, dusted down and placed at the centre of psychology's academic mantelpiece as the jewel in its crown, just above the fireplace where current theories are slowly turning to ashes to become just quaint reminders of the power our ego once had to turn things on their head. This is no consolation to Reich though, it's no use having a pardon or being acquitted if you have already been hung, drawn and quartered. Society drove Reich insane and then legitimised its behaviour by claiming that he was 'mad' all along hence his 'crazy' theory, which justified not having to consider it and thus avoid change. That sounds familiar in ego terms.

The Final Implication

Earlier I discussed the possibility of a spiritual template that defines the physical body based on Plato's 'cave analogy', but that speculation went against all the Laws of Evolution. The alternative speculation and final implication accepts the laws of evolution as one of the fundamental principles of the Universe, but this leads to even more remarkable conclusions than the idea of a spiritual template. Given the two parameters, the laws of evolution and the spiritual circulation contained in the notion of the bodymind and the Chakra system, then there can only be one logical conclusion. I recognise that this next section is pure speculation on the nature of our origins and it assumes the existence of a spiritual system that has evolved and is contained within the human body that some of you may not accept.

If the secret meditation technique and the underlying bodymind or Yogic Philosophy of a spiritual Chakra system is a reality, then how did that spiritual structure evolve and for what purpose? The laws of evolution inform us that the spiritual system, if it exists, would have evolved from the physical body, based on the natural assumption that the physical body evolved first and not the other way round. But it makes no sense at all for a spiritual system to have evolved that is absolutely no use to us in this life except as a means of reaching the next. The only logical conclusion is that human evolution is far more advanced than we can begin to understand.

'Ontogeny recapitulates Phylogeny' is the Recapitulation Theory of Ernst Haeckel. Ontogeny is the growth and development of individual species and Phylogeny is the evolutionary history of a species. The theory is that as each species individually develops to adulthood it passes through the whole of the species' evolutionary development, from the single-celled organism to the adult. The theory has apparently been disproved, but it feels so intuitively true that I think they must have thrown the baby out with the bathwater. One only has to observe human development in the womb from conception to birth to watch the evolution of the human species taking place. Here the sperm and the ovum come together to conceive human life, which recapitulates what happened millions of years ago in the primeval sea when evolution first took off; three single-celled organisms, two already united for the mutual benefit of motion in the head and tail of the sperm, uniting with the third, the ovum, in a mutuality that benefits all three. All this replicated in the primeval waters of the womb. The nine month gestation period corresponds to the period in evolution when life evolved in the sea and the moment of birth when we take our first breath of air corresponds to the moment when life crawled out of the sea onto land for the first time, and so on.

Projecting this idea back in time into our galaxy's history, the suggestion is that human life could have evolved on another planet very early in our galaxy's history, and human life has now evolved to a level beyond our comprehension to a spiritual being that can exist without a physical body. The possibility is that the very first human race evolved on a distant planet billions of years ago and ever since has been colonising the galaxy with the seeds of human life, and the Earth could be just one such colony. That original human race, after billions of years of evolution, could have evolved into a spiritual being that transcends physical matter. As one such colony of this advanced humanity we have inherited the spiritual framework on which existence without a physical body is possible. The development of the circulation of the light recapitulates that moment in the evolution of the original human race when they first developed that ability. This spiritual framework would thus appear and act like a spiritual template leading us on to a spiritual existence that intuitively spiritual archetypes tell us is a reality.

Just as a butterfly grows from a caterpillar, so millions of years of evolution take place in a matter of a few weeks inside the cocoon. The suggestion is that the human body is the equivalent of that cocoon, a tomb where millions of years of evolution should be taking place within us, and the development of our spiritual circulation is that evolution taking place over the eighty year period or so of our life, so that we may make the spiritual transition and take our place in the spiritual universe, the Kingdom of God, just like a butterfly.

In the secret process, the circulation of the light is like flying as a butterfly, riding a bike, galloping a horse, surfing a wave, one has to keep balance and ride with the process. One may keep falling off, but like any skill, practice makes perfect. Gnostics surf waves, they walk on water, turn water into wine, make water flow from a stone by striking it with a stick, raise the living from the dead, make the blind see and the deaf hear, ride a humble horse of God, baptise and suffer on the cross, but that does not mean they are a Messiah, they are just ordinary people like you and I. They also pull a sword from a stone and drink from the Holy Grail, but they do all these things spiritually, they are all well-known spiritual practices for a Gnostic. You can do them too, do not let your ego doubt your ability or deceive you. We do not need a new Messiah to set us free; you are your own Messiah, your own saviour, you have to set yourself free.

CHAPTER 5

Discussion and Conclusion

This conclusion is not going to be a balanced discussion and I make no apology for it being totally biased, because I am totally biased towards eternal human values and democratic principles. This is far too important a concept to contemplate introducing fair and equal debate. This is not a question of balance between good and evil, between right and wrong or the political left and right. There can be no halfway house compromise between eternal human values, democratic principles and the denial of them.

Gnostics developed the ability to directly experience God. This opened up within them the ability to grow spiritually and to become immortal. They tried to teach the world how to achieve this, but the world was not ready then, so they recorded the secret knowledge in code in the written word and in certain paintings and waited until humanity was ready to understand. I think that time has now arrived and Gnostics will feel free to come forward to guide us. The secret knowledge revealed in Poussin and Teniers' paintings is the process by which we can all have that direct experience of God ourselves. The ability to achieve this exists within our whole body consciousness, our bodymind based on the Yogic Chakra system which assumes the circulation of a vital energy, the light. The secret meditation technique enables us to use this system to access God and through that the opportunity for one's soul to grow, develop, mature and evolve into the real person you were meant to be, and to ultimately achieve the Holy Grail of an everlasting life. Our real self is that within us that has the potential to live on after physical death.

With this key to the secret knowledge it is possible to see that a wholly literal interpretation of the Bible is wrong, which has led to catastrophic consequences for millions of Christians who died believing they were saved when they were not. The real message from Jesus in the Bible is that we have to achieve our own salvation by our own efforts in this world, in this lifetime. This is the meaning contained in the Bible and the gospels, this is the meaning Jesus tried to convey to us, and this is the meaning of our life. Humanity is stuck at a very primitive level of development because the ego cannot accept that there is anything more than itself; "There is no other God but me," it cries out in its ignorance. The ego is a major obstacle to the process of spiritual growth. Its modus operandi is the use of the defence mechanisms of doubt, ridicule, denial, to disown, to reject, to mock and to project upon anything it does not understand, is frightened of or will lead to change in order to maintain its own selfish existence. The ego in its ignorance also prevents anyone else from straying too far from its chosen path with the powerful tool of social control, scapegoatism. The ego makes us all conform so that we all become united in our ignorance, it is scared stiff of being seen to be different in any way, but that means we all go down together. The ego is wantonly, arrogantly ignorant of, but pessimistic about human nature and its potential. Consequently, we have been lumbered with a Christian religion that is the opposite of what it claims to be and has become a barrier to God. We support a political system whose values are the opposite of the eternal human values we all pay lip service to. We have a dominant psychology which considers our unconscious to be a cesspit, when it is actually a treasure trove of beautiful gifts and opportunities, a psychotherapy that does not work because it does not treat the real problem and a psychiatry that treats the brain and thus only the symptoms of mental illness so can never effect a cure. On the world stage the ego is paranoid, but when challenged about this, accuses everyone else of being paranoid or a conspiracy theorist; it's called projection, but the ego is blind to its own activities.

I think another pattern has emerged here. The ego appears to have achieved a strange reversal of reality in all these cases. It reverses all our attempts to achieve eternal human values, it reverses the contents of the unconscious, it reverses the role of religion, it reverses the definition of freedom and the meaning of the word 'for', on the world stage it reverses the accusation of paranoia and creates the things it most fears, the ego sees what it wants to see. The ego performs a 'fait accompli', it blames the problem itself for the problem that the ego has created. Freud's unconscious cesspit is caused by the ego's repression of the treasure trove of human aspirations, perverts it, and then the ego blames it for being perverted, without realising that it is itself that has caused it to be that way. It reverses the motives of humanists, describing them as being agents of the devil when all they are trying to achieve is the same eternal human values as Jesus. Ironically, the ego is the agent of the devil that it accuses humanists of being. Religion is supposed to be our guide to God, but the ego has created a Christian Religion that has become a barrier to God by giving the responsibility for our salvation to bishops and priests and denying the reality of the true Jesus. The ego tells us that building a society based on eternal human values will not work because of human nature, but it is the ego by its repression that has created human nature in its own image. Human nature is not fixed for all time as we see it, the ego has caused it to be that way and society perpetuates it, but we can change human nature now that we have the means, we can free it and allow its goodness to come forth.

One only has to look at our own British society today to recognise these same processes in action. The ego blames the poor for being poor and living in poverty, even though it is the ego's capitalist system that creates poverty and keeps the poor poverty stricken. The ego blames the unemployed for not having a job even though the same system has caused the unemployment. The ego marginalises our children and then blames them for being a social problem when the real problem is the failure of capitalism to provide an equitable and just society for all. If one represses one's compassion and empathy for others then it becomes easy to blame the poor for blowing their money, to blame the unemployed for being lazy, to blame the uneducated for being thick, one does not even have to think about it, it is so obvious. The ego and capitalism would argue that the world does not owe people a living, but that is exactly wrong, the world does owe people 'a living'. We are your children, we did not ask to be brought into this world, the least we can expect from it is the opportunity to feed and clothe ourselves and our families with a roof over our heads, without losing our self-respect and dignity as a bare minimum requirement. Capitalism fails to provide these minimum requirements for all. The ego and capitalism create all these problems and then blame the problem it has created. We are your children's children, we were given all the material things we could possibly want but were left with a world that was spiritually bankrupt. We look for the possibility of a better, safer world in the future, but find ourselves governed by an economic system that is all powerful yet vulnerable to the vagaries of an open market, pursuing only that which is profitable, with no long term planning for the future of humanity. We are your children's children yet to be born, we do not know the place we are going, we accept it in good faith, we hope the world we enter will be kind, loving and compassionate, a place that is secure and safe for us to grow and to flourish, because if not, then that would be hell.

What Gnostics demonstrate so very eloquently is how foolish we all are to take the Bible literally. They play on our ignorance, they take the piss, and we don't even notice and in doing so make an important point about human nature at its most primitive level: that the ego is blind to the bleeding obvious. The individual and society need to pay attention to how the ego misleads us, how it deceives us, how our thinking, our ego consciousness, in its ignorance gets it wrong and in doing so limits our possibilities, e.g. any attempt to bring about a fair and just society based on the natural striving of the soul is thwarted by a pessimistic ego that believes we are all naturally evil and need protecting from ourselves; but that pessimistic ego has got it exactly wrong, our soul is full of natural goodness waiting to be released from its prison, the prison of a pessimistic mind-set. The ego has got away lightly so far, it is so confident that it will not be found out because it can always blame something else, it's called projection. We need to keep an eye on our ego's activity, agenda and goals and observe how the ego has made the world in its own image. As above so below, the ego created capitalism and now capitalism creates the type of ego it requires, in *its* own image. The collective ego is the capitalist economic and political system. Do not be fooled into believing that capitalism is the same as democracy. The ego wants you to believe that any attack on capitalism is an evil attack on our democratic way of life, the work of the devil. It's another neat, illusory trick, capitalism has hijacked democracy and hides its true nature behind it. Capitalism only tolerates democracy because it serves its purpose at this moment in time.

The devil does not really exist as a physical or spiritual entity. We have created the devil ourselves and have made a social construct that serves a specific social function. The devil is everything bad about us that we cannot accept in ourselves, that the ego represses by projecting it on to something else, in this case the devil. The devil gets a bad press, it is the scapegoat for all the evil within society, it is the ego and society's way of avoiding change. All the bad things that happen in society are blamed on evil individuals, "but there but for the grace of God go I". The concept of the devil allows society to avoid change by blaming individual acts of evil and not the real cause of the problem, a malfunctioning society. 'The devil' concept circumvents the real issue which is the way society avoids taking responsibility for its own actions by blaming something else, it's that projection thing again.

Gnostics depicted the devil as a goat with horns and cloven hooves specifically for this reason. They observed the ancient tradition in the Middle East whereby a goat upon whose head the sins of the villagers were symbolically placed was then sent out into the wilderness to die, taking their sins with it. This is the origin of the word 'scapegoat'. It is an irrational superstitious tribal custom, but which serves an important social function. It allows the status quo to survive without change and avoids conflict within the tribe of villagers. There is a direct comparison here with the behaviour of Jesus who went into the wilderness for forty days and then apparently died for our sins. The devil and Jesus are the ultimate scapegoats. The scapegoat, the devil and Jesus play the same role for society, they allow everyone else to avoid taking responsibility for their own sins and thus avoiding change. "Jesus died for our sins." We have literally projected all our sins on to Jesus and then sent him out into the wilderness eventually to die for us, just like the scapegoat. We have turned Jesus into a literal scapegoat and he plays the modern day equivalent for us that the goat did for those superstitious villagers. Unless of course this was not meant to be interpreted literally. The literal, irrational, superstitious belief denies the reality of the real Jesus who exists within each and every one of us as the potential to live on after physical death.

Our emotions and feelings, our soul, the unconscious, are like a little orphan, something cast out, rejected, unwanted, disowned by our ego, sent out into the wilderness, just like Jesus and the scapegoat, taking all the sins of the ego with it. The 'black sheep' of the family, or should that be the black 'goat', sent out so that the ego and society or the family can remain unchanged, but it is we who have to change. We have to change our superstitious understanding of spirituality, shake off the medieval 'mumbo jumbo', firstly by recognising it. Open your spiritual eyes and ears and understand in a completely different way. If the devil does exist then it is only in the concept of anything that acts as a barrier preventing us from reaching God. The ego and the collective ego of capitalism are already two candidates, but ironically also included are the Catholic Church, the Church of England, the Pope and all the Archbishops, Cardinals, Bishops, Priests, Vicars and the Jesus they have created who are all unwitting agents of that devil.

Capitalism is like a cuckoo in the nest of our democracy and the New Jerusalem our parents tried to build. They were fooled into accepting it, into feeding it, into working for it, and catering for its ever more demanding needs. It has a ravenous appetite, they worked all hours of the day to satisfy its hunger. They thought it was one of us, working for the same goals, the New Jerusalem, but we do not have the same aims, its hunger is for profits. It pretends to be one of us, but it is alien to the ultimate aim of our spirit and soul. It has pushed out and marginalised our children, the unemployed, the poor, the weak and the uneducated, leaving them with no prospects, and then fools us into blaming them and ignoring them while they starve. We feed its voracious appetite and it grows fat on our labour, and when it is finished with us it will fly the nest and move on like a multi-national company to find its next victim. The cuckoo that is capitalism has to be tamed also, the political system we deserve has to serve the people and not be their master.

The ego has to be reined in and its animal nature controlled, we need to become more self-aware and see the ego for what it is, our base animal instinct that is ignorant, fearful, arrogant, selfish, greedy, close-minded, pessimistic, doubting, smug, proud, paranoid, vindictive, jealous and a tyrant. Ironically, it is all those things that the ego accuses our unconscious of being. The ego is the cesspit that our ego warns us about, it is blind to itself. The ego thinks it is so civilised, so sophisticated, so intelligent, but it knows the price of everything and the value of nothing and remains a savage beast just beneath the surface, just a naked ape. Take away the thin veneer of society and the ego would descend into barbarity. The ego has to be tamed, it has to serve you and not be your master, it has to serve your spiritual purpose.

Capitalism has to be reined in before it destroys the world. In political debate it has always been possible to defeat capitalism on moral and environmental grounds. Capitalism is wastefully eating up the world's finite resources at an increasing and an alarming rate; what happens when the oil runs out? But now, since the financial crisis, capitalism can be defeated on economic grounds, because it has become clearly apparent just how precarious our economic system really is, it is subject to the regular affliction of 'boom and bust'. The economy appears to be built like a house of cards, rather like the ego, the slightest lack of confidence brings it all crashing down. "So what's wrong with a bit of healthy self-interest?" I hear you Tories cry. Well, greed and pessimism are, because self-interested greed creates the boom and self-interested pessimism the bust. Everything is fine whilst confidence in the economy is high when our greedy ego self-interest gets sucked up into a confidence spiral boom of ever more lucrative returns on investments; but when the economy becomes so overstretched that a loss of confidence sets in and the bubble bursts the inevitable ego's pessimism takes over and the problems of an unregulated economic system emerge, and from that moment the economy is doomed to bust and all of us with it, as a 'healthy self- interest' tries to save its own skin. Is this behaviour rational, that our ego's fear should bring about the one thing it is most afraid of and bankrupt the nation? It may be logical human behaviour to try to save one's skin, but it is not rational human behaviour to bring the whole economy to its knees. This may be one of the few occasions when logic and rationalism do not coincide.

Gordon Brown was a first rate Chancellor of the Exchequer, a brilliant economist and all the top economic spokesmen agreed on this at the time. He guaranteed an end to 'boom and bust', he promised the nation it would never happen again and he will always be remembered for those inopportune words. But there is something strangely odd about the over-confidence shown by all parties at the time. All the top economists from the top schools of economics who begrudgingly agreed on Brown's competence, could not envisage the bust occurring, but is this not what economists are supposed to be able to foresee, what use are they otherwise? It caught them all by surprise, they could not anticipate it even though history could have predicted it would happen at some point. It is as if some missing factor has been left out of the economists' equations, a gremlin in the system that strikes at random, some invisible phenomenon that economists are not aware of, that they are not only blind to, but blind to even though they know it's coming and will probably happen at some point in the future, an 'x' factor, human emotions. You know emotions, they are those awkward little things that always seem to get in the way of scientific experiments on human behaviour, if . . . etc. The same factor that is missing from psychological theories is also missing from economic theories, this gremlin has feelings. But the collective ego which is capitalism gets off scot free again by blaming individual greedy bankers and not the capitalist system that spawns them. The ego persuades us that everything would be fine if it wasn't for just a few 'rogue traders', but "there but for the grace of God go I, again".

The capitalist system is like a conjuring trick that works on the principle of fiscal illusion. As long as the money keeps circulating nobody seems to notice the shortfall, but as soon as the 'gravy train' stops, the illusion becomes clear and blind panic sets in. Boom and bust is cyclical and an inevitable part of a capitalist system and the busts occur regularly every thirty or so years. Ironically, capitalism will never work because of 'human nature being what it is', because of the ego's greed and pessimism, it will always succumb to boom and bust, that's the nature of 'the beast'; it's time to get this cuckoo out of our nest. Humanity has to develop a new social, political and economic order, one that is stable, not subject to boom and bust and not based on the capricious whims of investors, or vulnerable to a paranoid ego, one not based on selfish greed but on selfless compassion, and an optimism about the economy even when times are hard. Would that not be the wise thing to do? We can do it now we have the means.

There is one more crime against humanity the ego stands accused of: the ego will not allow humanity to flourish and evolve, because the ego does not like change, it is very 'conservative' by nature. The core of the problem is that society cannot agree on what social progress is, how or in which direction to proceed or even whether we need to change, progress or grow at all, except financially of course. Successive governments in Britain of both the right and the left have only ever envisaged human progress in physical and financial terms. Why have we allowed that assumption to go unchallenged? The effectiveness of a political system seems to be judged solely on its financial success. Why? Who has decided that this is the best criteria for assessing the success of a nation? What about our education? A harmonious society? Our children's safety? Our children's prospects? The elderly? Caring for those less fortunate than ourselves? The sick? Employment in a useful rewarding job? Reduction in crime? Affordable homes for all? These are all measures of a civilised society and all of these things bring with them dignity and a respect for oneself and others, and improve the quality of people's lives. Aren't all these things a better measure of success? Judged by these criteria, Britain's success as a nation is an abject failure. The world we have allowed the ego and capitalism to create is exactly the wrong way round in human terms, a mirror image of the reality that humanity strives for, those eternal and absolute human aspirations contained in the concept of a spiritual reality. Capitalism has to be replaced eventually with a new political and economic system, one that values the spirit and soul and acknowledges the growth and development of humanity as its first priority. Britain had a chance to lead the world to its first Socialist Arcadia, but we lost our way after 1945 because our ego thinking, our head, that extraordinary brilliant brain, was corruptible.

Social progress and political issues seem to be cyclical in nature rather like 'boom and bust'. Any progress or political achievements made by optimists are soon clawed back when the political reaction of pessimists sets in, e.g. in the past forty years, progress in education, in social services, in mental health, in trade unionism and politics, all clawed back. Next, women's rights? Sometimes political progress seems like running forwards on a conveyor belt going backwards, as soon as you slow down or stop making progress you end up back exactly where you started. Does society move towards the left and become more liberated, more tolerant of others, more compassionate, more progressive or does society move towards the right and become more conservative, more selfish, more money orientated and none of the above things? It would be helpful if people could agree on a political system that would be acceptable to all. During the 20th century and in living memory there were two competing political philosophies in Britain, Capitalism and Socialism, represented by the Conservative and the Labour Parties respectively. The problem with these two competing political philosophies is that there was no meeting point between them, no halfway house compromise, there can be no common ground between two diametrically opposed ways of organising society; consequently any gains by Tories were clawed back by Socialists and any progress by Socialists were clawed back by the Tories, the net result stalemate and the stagnation of humanity. It is self-evident that humanity needs a humanitarian political party based on eternal human values and principles, if only for our children's sake, it is so obvious we shouldn't even need to think about it, but the ego will not let society move in that direction because it is frightened of political change, it likes things to stay just as they always have been. It would be nice if we were able to agree on a political philosophy so we could all pull together, but first we have to agree that progress should not be gauged solely in financial terms, but also in human terms. This is no longer a question of the political left or the political right, of a choice between Socialism and capitalism, this is an issue of the striving of our spirit and soul for absolute eternal human values and principles and the denial of them. The political choice for humanity is between progress and stagnation, to the left is human progress, growth and development of the soul and to the right stagnation of the soul and the denial of humanity.

Let me be quite clear what I'm saying here, humankind has reached a political fork in the road, to the right a selfish greedy future based on the physical world where money, possessions, power, privilege and status rule and the logical progression of which leads to a pure-bred race of super-humans and to hell with the hindmost, perfect physical specimens with super-brains and super-intelligence, but who are not really 'human' at all. To the left a future based on the eternal humanitarian values of justice, truth, equality, freedom, love, compassion and empathy for one another where our spirit and soul can flourish, blossom and become immortal. In order to evolve spiritually, humankind has to stop worshipping the literal, physical and financial world and start contemplating the spiritual, eternal human principles and values. Which way, the head or the heart? You must decide.

You would now probably expect me to declare that Socialism is the answer to all our problems, but not without qualification. Socialism may be a good starting point and a marker for what could be achievable, but the political direction humanity has to embark upon exists above the one dimensional political bickering of Left, Right or Centre politics. This is no longer a choice of left, right or centre, this is a choice between progress for humanity or stagnation. This new political direction exists above the malaise of current politics on a different plane and would help us all to rise above it, a new direction that values emotions, feelings, the spirit and soul and the growth of humanity above anything else. The future of humanity lies in a 'socialism of the heart' not the head, and women must take the lead in this because they remain more in touch with their emotions and feelings. The head, our thoughts can be corrupted, a honest heart never can. Humanity will succeed or fail based on this straight choice, the feminine nurturing aspect is humanity's only hope. We all need to unite around this endeavour for the sake of our children's future and for humanity. We need to decide on a new political philosophy by freeing the soul and letting it choose a system that will allow it to flourish. We also need just a little of Eve's wisdom.

The ego has been found wantonly guilty of the crime of wilful neglect of the orphan of humanity by pursuing financial incentives, more and more possessions, status, privilege, power and a hedonistic lifestyle whilst this orphan starves, remains homeless, unemployed, at the same time denying any other possibilities and at the expense of the quality of its children's lives. The sentence will be commensurate with the crime. The ego shall be taken from this place forthwith and placed in solitary confinement, living only on scraps and morsels, until in time some form of rehabilitation can be achieved, at which point the ego will be freed in order to serve its new master, the soul, its own orphan, until the end of time.

We are all pirate ships on the sea of life, each seeking our own treasure. The soul is like a keel, without one you can sail faster but are blown off course by the prevailing wind. The soul is a heavy burden, like a keel it slows you down, but you are not blown off your true course. It may take you longer to get there, longer to learn things because you have to feel them with your heart. The soul makes one appear slow, foolish and naïve, it embarrasses you in company, it makes you do things that appear stupid and weak, it made you make that loud noise when everyone else was quiet, it misunderstood that simple instruction. Your ego repressed your soul because your soul made it look stupid. Your ego cast your soul out into the wilderness because it was protecting itself from ridicule. Nobody wants to look stupid, to be the odd one out, to be made the scapegoat. The ego will do anything to avoid becoming the object of ridicule even if it has to join the safety in numbers of a clique whose main weapon is ridicule if you do not toe the line. Scapegoating is a very powerful means of social control, people see how the scapegoat is treated and will do anything to avoid the same fate even if that means dropping one's values and principles and abandoning one's soul. Scapegoatism is the last great 'ism' that society has to address; it is like racism, an ego defence mechanism which projects onto others that which it cannot accept in itself, in this case to be different. Scapegoatism is an insidious bullying type of defence mechanism because in order to avoid it you have to do it to others pre-emptively. We do it, we know we do it and then we deny we do it. It is another neat trick that society needs to make totally transparent. This is what you may have to face if you choose to undertake the secret process, if you go back and rescue that abandoned child within you, you may be made to play the role of the scapegoat for being different. Have faith in that small part of yourself, it is stronger than you think, have a brave heart, if you become the scapegoat, be contented that you are on course, and with courage you will arrive there first on your treasure island, Arcadia.

Our parents had a dream, it was the same dream that Martin Luther King had, it is a recurring dream that one day people will build a world based on eternal human values, and be "free at last". That dream was stolen from us, not by stealth in the middle of the night, but right before our eyes when we watched the greatest American President JFK assassinated live on television and not long after that Martin Luther King was sniped from a rooftop. These were great men and they inspired a generation because they embodied all our hopes and dreams for a better world, and were killed because of that. In Britain we do things slightly differently, we do not shoot the politicians who might bring about real change, we assassinate their characters, much more civilised, less messy, thoroughly British, and who can prove a thing?

We, the baby boomer generation, allowed all this to happen, whilst we were being seduced by the accumulation of more and more possessions and selfishly pursuing everything that the consumer society could provide us with. Everything seemed fine whilst the gravy train was still rolling, but now it has stopped, the seduction is revealed as a fiscal sleight of hand, the equivalent of 'spot the pea under the pot'. The illusion is, the pea is irrelevant, you should have been keeping your eye on the pot, when the economy stops, the scam is, 'spot where your pension pot went'. It is a grand illusion and we are the suckers who are left with nothing. We fell for it all and provided nothing in return for the next generation, our children, and in the process have allowed the world to move nearer to self-destruction.

We have to consider the long term development of the human race. Greed and selfishness may be needed to 'oil' the wheels of capitalism in the short term, but as a long term proposition greed and selfishness are not human traits to be encouraged. We need to build for the future of our children and design a system that can make the transition from a selfish, uncaring, exclusive society to one that is compassionate and inclusive. This should be the long term goal of any civilised society. We need a new truly Spiritual Church, a new approach to psychology, psychotherapy and psychiatry and a new Social, Political and Economic order based on eternal human values and democratic principles, with an optimism about human nature and the contents of the unconscious.

You now know the Great Secret, you know the secret of Rennes le Chateau and the D.M. code, you know what the Holy Grail is, where to find it and how to drink from it, and you know what the Spear of Destiny is. You know the Meaning of Life and how to attain everlasting life not in this world but the next. I give you the key to the door of a great treasure, your bodymind contains that treasure, it is contained within your unconscious, a treasure trove of secret wisdom and beautiful gifts from God, a coat of many colours. All of this is your 'soul' inheritance, it belongs to you only, but you have to claim it. I give you the key to the door of the Kingdom of God, I give you the key to the door to yourself, God is within you, within that little abandoned orphan child of humanity, I give you the key; now don't lose it again.

Some may say, "We should not allow this secret knowledge to get into the hands of the wrong sort of people", which usually means into the hands of ordinary people. But the truth is classless and should never be concealed, anyway the poor have a much better chance of reaching the Kingdom of God than the rich, the secret knowledge may be wasted on a rich elite. But I have every faith in the transformational nature of the secret process, so throw away those Jimmy Choo's, that Cartier watch, sell that Ferrari and give the money to the poor, open up your luxury house to the homeless, go help out at the night-shelter and learn some humility, get a job, or work voluntarily in the caring services and put something back into society. You do not need those possessions, they are of no use to you now. There is nothing more important in the world than this; this is it. Every living soul should be given this one chance, this one shot, this one opportunity, this is your inheritance, your legacy bequeathed to you by God, are you going to capture it, or just let it slip?

The Great Secret is the knowledge of the Way to directly experience God and through that to achieve immortality. You now have the key, you know where the door is, you only have to turn the lock and open the door. I am here to reassure you that there is nothing to be afraid of except your fear of change itself. Is this a hoax or not a hoax? You have to decide, only you can do that, don't listen to anyone else, you have to decide this one yourself. Am I the agent of Beelzebub or is it your ego? Listen to your heart, your thoughts will deceive you, follow your star, let your Daemon Guardian Angel guide you, let it be your helper, your soul won't be led astray. Have faith in the potential of your soul's inner wisdom, but to do that you have to let go, your ego has to let go of control. There is nothing to lose except that which is worthless and everything to gain that is priceless. This is the moment when you have to decide, to open the door or not to open the door, that is the question.

This is my gift to my children and the next generation, it is too late for my generation, but you can make a better world based on those eternal human values and democratic principles. Time is running out for all of us, keep an eye on your ego and on the 'cuckoo that is capitalism'; control your ego, don't let it control you, control capitalism don't let it destroy the world. They are the Demiurge, the gods of this world, the real enemy of the people, the real enemy within, the Anti-Christ. Choose a fairer political system for your children to grow up under, one that will not ravage the planet, one that will not demonise your children, but nurture them and educate them in a safe society where we all pull together for the common good, and nobody is marginalised or discriminated against because they are different. Choose a system that will allow our spiritual nature to thrive and not be enslaved to our ego and to capitalism. That doesn't sound too much to ask, does it? Shouldn't we all have been striving for that anyway? Ask yourself what it was that stopped us. We failed, but you can do this now you have the means, you can change human nature now you have the key, it is not permanently fixed, you can build a brave new world, a new New Jerusalem, Arcadia.

The ego will try to convince you that God is a delusion, because it knows there can be no proof, thus confirming its own omnipotence. I cannot prove to you that God exists, I have only my own personal experience and that is no proof to anyone but me, and if I am deluded then welcome to my delusion, only you can decide. Listen to your heart, delusion is a malfunctioning of our thinking, a thought disorder, it is our ego thinking that leads us astray and into delusion. Descartes got it exactly wrong because of his head centred mind-set, he should have stated, "I *feel* therefore I am. I think therefore I *am not.*" You have to experience God yourself to know of God's reality, the challenge is there for everyone, you have to take it, what are you afraid of, becoming deluded? If so, then I thoroughly recommend this delusion to everyone, not all of us get the opportunity to undermine both Freud and Descartes in the same breath, and opportunities like this are endless, there is a whole new world out here waiting for you to take the risk.

There is some indirect evidence that God exists; firstly, the probability that we have an advanced and highly evolved spiritual system contained within our bodymind that is of no practical use to us in this existence except as a means of reaching a possible next. Secondly, the notion that the rich cannot buy their way into God's Kingdom is so beautifully subtle, such sublime justice that some higher wiser power has to exist if only for us to be able to congratulate it on its brilliance. Thirdly, God is an energy that fills the entire Universe, it is there but we cannot see it, like dark matter.

It could be that Gnostics and physicists are both describing the same thing from an entirely different point of view. God is all around us; we exist in God like a fish exists in water, but the ego has created a capsule that does not let God in and so we slowly expire, like a fish with no gills. We have to learn to use our spiritual gills, our chakras, so that we may live in God and become immortal. And finally of course, and you might find this surprising because this is what we have been told all along and have chosen not to see it; God is love. God exists in our emotions, our feelings, our unconscious, the orphan that we reject and disown, sent out into the wilderness to wither and die on the vine. Love is the pinnacle of our emotions and feelings and if you can experience true love you will know God. You have to be brave enough to experience love before you can reject God. This Universe is filled with love, but we all have to be courageous enough to let it in, to let God into our hearts. We experience God as we experience love. Love *is* our experience of God. The question is; is our experience of love just a delusion? Millions of years ago life made the transition from sea to land by evolving the ability to breathe in air; we now need to take our next evolutionary leap by utilising our potential to breathe in God. And we all know what happened to the fish that laughed at the frog for believing in air, it's stuck in the sea still denying the reality of any other way of being. Fish thought frog was deluded, but frog didn't need to prove air existed in order to be able to experience it, and it did not matter how much frog tried to explain to fish what air was like, frog neither had the words, nor fish the means of understanding or any reason to believe, until one day, suddenly and without warning, the pond dried up, and then, for a few sad moments, fish understood. In the end it does not matter what atheists, sceptics or fish believe, evolution is leading us inexorably on towards God whether we like it or not.

Every so often the human race likes to scare itself to death by entering into a mass contagious paranoid panic. Paranoid panics are very similar to Professor Stuart Hall's moral panics, but without the moral element. Paranoid panics are the modern day equivalent of the prediction that 'the end of the world is nigh'. In the recent past we have had the herpes scare, the AIDS scare, the SARS scare, mad cow disease scare, the swine flu scare and the bird flu scare, on any number of counts I should be dead already, but obviously I am not, I just wait for the next paranoid panic to worry myself to death about. We will probably all die of heart disease brought on by all this worrying. So what's going on here, do you not think we should have got wise to these events by now, or is the bogey man eventually going to get us? One could almost begin to predict the next arrival, we should be due another one quite soon now; watch this space. Surely there is a new science here, how about the History of the Paranoid Panic or Doomongerology? Do you not think that these panics tell us more about ourselves than they do about the world around us.

The issue of global warming is an example of how the ego probably misleads us, based on paranoid hysteria. The debate on global warming has reached an intensity in which the language used has developed a religious fervour in which the two sides are described as believers and deniers, and the deniers have become the modern day heretics and any attempt by them to present the alternative viewpoint is considered blasphemy, and which will in all likelihood turn into a witch-hunt. Why does the debate have to descend to this level of abuse? We should be able to discuss these issues rationally without having to resort to hectoring, surely the truth is more important than who wins the argument. This particular paranoid panic has reached a hysterical frenzy where no-one wants to be the odd one out, the scapegoat, nobody wants to be a denier, so everyone toes the believer's line. Both sides have valid arguments, but neither side seems to want to see the other's point of view, e.g. with increased levels of carbon dioxide in the atmosphere one would expect the greenhouse effect to lead to an increase in the temperature of the Earth, but the geological evidence contradicts that. The believers remain adamant that the deniers are wrong even in the face of the only genuine relevant long term study and indisputable evidence there is. This is a rather odd reaction, an interesting social phenomenon, whereby believers ignore the most significant evidence and then follow the prevailing fashionable consensus of opinion.

My argument is not for one side or the other on this issue, this discussion is about the nature of disagreement itself. Two people can see the same evidence and then come to different conclusions, e.g. the left and right in politics. This discussion is also about the nature of truth itself; just how many truths can there be? Surely there can be only one accurate conclusion, the truth, based on all the evidence at the time. If one has not got all the relevant evidence then there may be an excuse for not reaching the right conclusion and which can be rectified at a later date with the arrival of some new evidence. But when strong evidence that is already known, is ignored, then there can be no excuse for reaching the wrong conclusion.

It appears that on this earthly plane we have all been condemned to disagree on practically everything, and one wonders how humanity can ever progress or evolve at all. How is it possible for us to disagree on so many issues? The answer is, of course, the ego is blind to the bleeding obvious. Is it that the ego cannot see, does not want to see, or it suits its purpose not to see? We are right back at that concept of seeing with spiritual eyes and hearing with spiritual ears again; to be able to see the spirit of the law and not just the letter of the law; to be able to understand with our hearts and not just our heads, e. g. if you want an example of how the letter of the law subverts the spirit of the law then look no further than the copyright law with regards to Teniers painting. The problem seems to be that we all appear to disagree on the letter of the law, and tend to get bogged down in the detail and fall out over the minutiae of everyday life and the many different truths that exist at this level of understanding. If we could all see the bigger picture, the intention behind the letter of the law, the spirit of the law, then we may all be able to see that there is only one real truth, which will allow us all to agree on a course of action. We have to be able to rise above these petty basic conflicts of self-interest and judge them objectively with wisdom, based on a new higher spiritual level of understanding, compassion and empathy, and recognise that the ego, as well as being a deceitful little git, is an obstacle to this process and needs isolating first, before any progress can be made.

The nature of disagreement is like two people playing a tennis match, but unbeknown to them both, they are not playing together on the same court. Consequently each player serves a good argument but no return is received so both sides think they are winning, but no point is made. Perhaps both players should agree beforehand which court they will be playing on, and what time, and then perhaps they would be able to have a decent game of cut and thrust debate, with an eventual winner based on the skill and logic of their argument. I suggest that the court that both players should always be playing on is the spirit of the law, rather than the letter of the law tennis court, which is notoriously slippery, with uneven bounce, markings unclear, the wrong way round and so easy to cheat on.

I do not think anyone would seriously argue that the human race has not caused untold pollution to the environment and immeasurable damage to the delicate fabric and balance of nature, but this is a separate issue to global warming, and they may or may not be related. The ego has probably got it exactly wrong again, but it does not matter now who wins the argument, now that the issue has been raised, doing nothing is not an option, critically, the future of our planet is at stake, we cannot wait to see if the deniers were right all along, it could be too late by then, as long as we realise that it may in the end turn out to have been totally unnecessary; at least we will leave a less polluted world to our children. But why can't believers say this and why can't deniers understand this?

On the issue of the paranoid panic our ego thinking gets it wrong and continues to get it wrong. I shall really start to worry when the next pandemic arrives and the ego says, "Don't worry, there's nothing to be afraid of, it's harmless", or perhaps we will all get caught out like the boy who cried wolf. But the ego never stops to reflect and question its own actions, it just carries on regardless in self-denial until the next paranoid panic, the next 'end of the world is nigh' scenario, when the ego will get it exactly wrong again and we will all have to toe the paranoid believer's line again. Our ego thinking is supposed to be completely rational and never deluded, so how does one explain the above? From this evidence it is clear that our ego thinking can be deluded and irrational at times such as these, and gets it exactly wrong most of the time based on projection, greed, paranoia, self- interest and short term fixes without any consideration for the long term. The debate on global warming illustrates the kind of bullying conformity that Gnostics had to face and which eventually drove them underground rather than renounce their beliefs; this attitude they had to face was one of bullying authoritarianism that is becoming worryingly prevalent again in today's society. But it also illustrates why we need to become more self-aware of our own and others' ego behaviours and attitudes and of the type of social pressure that is applied to us all by subtle means in order to make us conform to the majority point of view, e.g. the use of the pejorative word 'denier' as in, "you're not a *denier* are you?" Anyway, usually in these circumstances the majority are nearly always wrong.

The main thing to grasp, if you have not done so already, and I am in danger of repeating myself here, is that human nature is not fixed for all time, it is only this way because this is how the ego has created us, by repressing our natural emotional vitality with muscular tensions. Our potential was infinite, but our ego skewed us in a certain direction so that we would fit neatly into society and not be the odd one out. We were forced to repress certain emotions and feelings from a very early age, remember how it was never the 'done thing' to show emotions, especially if the neighbours could hear, and these types of continuing subtle repressions created our permanent character for the rest of our lives which became the national characteristics, e.g. the baby that is left to cry itself to sleep when all it wanted was reassurance; the baby that is potty trained too early so that, instead of gaining control of its anal sphincter in the natural way, it has to tense all the muscles in that area, creating a mean-spirited person, a 'tight arse'. Ask yourself how we justified doing those things? What did we think we were trying to achieve? Remember that relationship that broke your heart and you vowed never to be hurt again, the problem is once you turn your emotions off it is difficult to turn them back on again and you end up hurting someone who perhaps did not deserve it, and so it goes, round and round. We pay lip service to love and yet very few of us have retained the ability, or possess the courage to allow ourselves to experience true love, the ego won't let us take that risk and so we settle for a sentimental and sanitised version; it's safer. Our developmental possibilities were endless, but our ego limited us to just one narrow specific channel so that we became the same as everyone else, selfish, greedy, pessimistic, emotionless personalities with no compassion or empathy for others, perfect little compliant units of labour to service the capitalist system, and the mechanism that allows the ego to achieve that by cutting off our emotions is muscular tensions, the chains that bind us as we all go down together. We are all like little creatures hiding in our shells, afraid to come out for fear of being attacked as the scapegoat, but there is nothing to be afraid of out here except your own fear itself. It's time to stop armouring yourself against the fear and pain of life and cast off that armour shell, those chains that bind you, and open yourself up to the Universe. To a Gnostic, the human body is like a tomb of our own making, as depicted in Poussin's painting, in which we are all trapped, unable to find a way out. The secret key opens the door to your spiritual tomb to let you *out*, this is how you are raised from the dead, raised from being spiritually dead to become spiritually alive. Religion may have been the opium of the masses, but ironically, it is our spirituality that will finally set us free. We can break free from the legacy of that rigid limiting socialisation process now, and take control of our own development, set *ourselves* free and become individuals who live outside 'the box', "free at last".

A seven year old child had such compassion for others that they wondered how much more compassionate must the grown up world be? Sadly, seven is when the ego kicks in. You probably think I have been very hard on your ego, just a tad, but this was only to make the point as strongly as I could. I do realise that the ego is only doing what it has to do to help you survive in a god-forsaken world. I can't be hard enough on capitalism, but your ego's big mistake is to accept the status quo as it finds it without question and not to realise that it has a lot more potential than it thinks. Your ego isn't all bad really, it is doing the best it can under impossible circumstances. It is not a complete imposter, a demon, your twin or a git and it does not entirely die, there remains a core element that will remain a continuing part of your developing personality. These are just Gnostic ways of presenting the underlying dynamics of the bodymind, analogies of fundamental psychological issues that take place within us; they turn these facets of our personality into characters in order to discuss the dynamics, to make a spiritual point. Your ego is you at a basic fundamental and primitive level, a naked ape, at its most appealing, a lovable rogue or the whore with a heart of gold, Mary Magdalene; at its least appealing a psychopath.

King Arthur was a hero the same as Jesus. Arthur's Knights of the Round Table were just different facets of his own personality, the same as the Apostles were for Jesus. Lancelot was Arthur's soul, Guinevere his spirit. Arthur, the purified ego, realised he had to die so they could live, united together as one. The sword in the stone is a direct reference to the secret spiritual process, you must pull the sword from your own stone to start the process. Your soul loves your ego unconditionally, warts and all, but your ego does not even know of your soul's existence, "there is no other god but me". You will have to introduce them because this is the basis of the greatest eternal love story ever told, *Beauty and the Beast, Romeo and Juliet, Arthur and Guinevere*. Unfortunately, your ego, in its ignorance, keeps your soul imprisoned at a basic level and will not allow it to develop into the person that you potentially are because it is afraid of the unknown. The ego has to be taken to task and its eyes opened to its own behaviour and attitude, an egocentric attitude on the individual scale and an ethnocentric attitude on a national scale. If we could persuade our ego to be less egocentric, to become more self-aware of its own attitudes then we could avoid projecting uncomfortable feelings onto others, and face up to the unpleasant truths that exist within ourselves. Projection, ultimately, is a denial of truth within ourselves, leading to a reversal of reality which makes us blind to the suffering of others, blind to the real cause of suffering and injustice in the world, blind to the real meaning of Jesus, blind to any other possibilities and blind to itself and its own behaviour. We have to stop blaming everyone else, and face up to these uncomfortable truths, we have to stop hiding from them and courageously emerge from our shells, from Plato's cave. You have to convince your ego there is nothing to be afraid of and a whole new world out here waiting for you to "come forth, Lazarus".

Gnostics gained access to God by a secret method of prayer that bypassed the ego's constant vigilance. They did this through a highly evolved spiritual system, which remains 'dormant' in most people within the bodymind, the Chakra system. The Chakra system is where our soul resides and is the means of achieving direct contact with God. The soul should naturally develop through the Chakras as it matures, evolves and grows towards the Light of God, like a flower grows towards the light of the sun, each Chakra opening like a flower blooms, as our soul reaches that level, or like a vine, each Chakra developing like grapes on the vine. Jesus is the 'sun' of God that our soul aspires to, not the 'son' of God. The 'son of God' is a literal misunderstanding based on a Gnostic play on words. The Chakras are our soul's stairway to heaven; the soul exists within our Chakra system and wants to grow, but your ego is scared of letting that happen. Your ego is only doing what it thinks it has to do to help you survive in the world in which it finds itself. Your soul has to gently persuade your ego that it needs help, that it has to let go and make way for something better to come. The ego is what we believe human nature to be naturally and permanently, however, the ego is only a very limited version of our true potential. Human nature can be changed for the better by bypassing the ego using the secret method of prayer and allowing our soul to grow in the 'Sun of God' to achieve the Holy Grail and spiritual immortality. This was the Gnostic heresy that became the Greatest Secret in the World and is the legacy that Gnostics became trustees to and custodians of.

All of this will happen one day, not in my generation or perhaps not even in the next, but one day everything in this book, which at the moment may seem far-fetched and unbelievable will in the future appear normal and common sense. It will happen because it is the truth, it is the truth whose bells ring out down through the ages, they are the chimes of freedom. The future will look back at us incredulously and wonder why we had so much difficulty grasping the obvious; why we were so blind to the truth; how we were able to turn a blind eye to the real cause of suffering in the world; why we were so lacking in compassion for each other; why it took us so long to break free from the grip of our egos and from capitalism; why we hung on for so long to such outdated medieval and superstitious religious notions; why we nearly destroyed the world. Right now we need to grasp the fact that we have to embrace change courageously in order for us to remain human. History will judge us on this moment. All of this will happen one day, and when it does, if we survive that long, historians will look back and say, "This was the start of it, this was the moment when the penny finally dropped, this was the spark that ignited a spiritual revolution." This was the time when humanity first truly recognised their own divine nature and realised their selfish animal nature would lead them into oblivion if not harnessed. This era marks the end of a primitive, medieval, supernatural and superstitious spiritual age and brings a new rational understanding to the life of the spirit in the 21st century to make it the most important endeavour in one's life, the meaning of one's life. If we survive the next 500 years, history will look back at your generation with relief and respectfully say, "This was our finest hour." This was one giant step for the individual, one tremendous leap for humanity.

I apologise if you have found my writing style irritating and patronising. Right from the start I faced a dilemma of how I should address the reader without sounding as though I were preaching. In the end I decided to speak directly from the heart as if talking to an equal individual and not pretend I don't know what I do know. The important thing is that this knowledge is out there, make of it what you will, if you think that I am an arrogant, irritating, patronising, condescending, pretentious little twit, that's fine, as long as you have understood what I have written. Someone had to call time, and I've seen enough.

Finally then and in conclusion, our emotions, our feelings, our spirit, our soul, the very things that make us most human, and the underlying basis for them, the potential within us to be more than we are, the ability to love unconditionally, the ability to experience God, the potential to live on after death, all these things are connected and interrelated, and all these things are rejected, ignored, denied and ridiculed by an ignorant, arrogant and pessimistic ego. The Gnostic Secret is that the Holy Grail and the Spear of Destiny are real spiritual phenomena, the attainment of which indicates the achievement of immortality, which is the Meaning of Life. This meditation technique allowed Gnostics to experience their soul through their emotions and feelings and by doing so to access Universal Wisdom. This was achieved through point **A** in the bodymind, and then by locating their centre of consciousness, their centre of being at point **B** in the bodymind as previously outlined. This technique allowed them to step 'out of the box' and objectively see the world as it really is, and from that vantage point it becomes apparent that human beings have created a world that is exactly the wrong way round in human terms, a mirror image of the eternal human values and aspirations that we all pay lip service to. It also became clear that human beings are not using their faculties to the full and remain at a very primitive developmental level, in an ignorant slumber, and our emotions and feelings, far from being superfluous and irrational, are the source of great wisdom and potential which could awaken us from that slumber. It also became clear that humanity, rather than growing and evolving, is actually stagnating and withering like grapes on the vine because our spirit and soul are enslaved to a political system that has no care for them. Emotions and feelings, the things that make us most human, are denigrated by capitalism, society, Academia, the Human Sciences and Religion. The agent of this strange reversal of reality is the ego which by projection refuses to see anything other than its own selfish existence and its own distorted mirror view of the world. The ego refuses to allow the soul to awaken, it keeps it 'unconscious', by denying the soul's existence, but the ego 'cuts its nose off to spite its face', together the ego and the soul could be infinitely greater than they are, as long as the ego recognises that there is another God and this God is far greater than it.

Human nature is not fixed for all time as we see it, the ego with the help of society repressed the infinite possibilities of our development and prevented us from being much more than we became. Our emotions and feelings are the means of accessing a massive source of wisdom and understanding and are full of infinite possibilities, and our rational ego thinking represents only the small part of the conscious whole that we were allowed to develop through the socialisation process in order to fit into society as it exists, the rest was repressed and became unconscious, 'the unconscious'. But we could have been much more than we were allowed to become, we were limited, handicapped, blinkered by that socialisation process, and it is all that which remains dormant within our unconscious that represents our true potential, the potential to grow in God's light and become immortal. What we became was a reflection of the selfish, greedy capitalist system into which we were born, a reflection of the rational world, just a pale reflection of what we could have been. That which is conscious, our ego thinking, our rationality, is all that we are left with, just 10% of our capacity. The rest, the 90% unconscious represents all that we can be, all that we were supposed to be, all that is our destiny. There is still 90% of yourself to explore, we should all be aiming for 100% consciousness, sod capitalism. We all have to explore our emotions and feelings and not be ashamed or scared of them.

The wisdom and understanding available to us through the unconscious 'lies there dormant', and the evidence for this lack is there for all to see, e.g. is it wise or rational to interpret the Bible literally? Is it wise or rational to accept without question medieval, superstitious and supernatural religious beliefs? Is it wise or rational to support an unjust and unfair political system? Is it wise or rational to invest everything in an economic system when we know it is unstable? Is it wise or rational to only see human progress in physical and financial terms? Is it wise or rational for the Human Sciences and Academia in general to ignore our emotions and feelings? Is it wise or rational to pursue power, status, privilege and possessions at any price and then go to Church on Sunday to be forgiven for one's sins? Is it wise or rational to elevate selfishness, greed and ruthlessness into virtues under the euphemism 'ambition'? Is it wise or rational to reverse reality and blame the problem and ignore the cause? Is it wise or rational to allow the ego to reverse the reality of human aspirations? Is it wise to dismiss an ancient spiritual system without exploring its claims? Is it wise not to believe in God? Is it wise to ridicule, deny and ignore these things? Is it wise to believe anything the ego tells us? Is it wise to believe me?

The head, our ego thinking, our extraordinary brilliant brain, our ever so clever intelligence has got it exactly wrong in human terms because we have all been socialised into dismissing our emotions and feelings as irrelevant and irrational, when in actual fact they are the most relevant and real things about us; consequently it has always failed to see 'the elephant in the room', the enormous potential contained within them. Surely it is inconceivable that throughout the entire history of the whole planet, the best minds, the greatest philosophers, the leading thinkers of the day, could all have got it so consistently and so spectacularly, exactly wrong. How can that be possible? We are rational people living in a rational world, how can this be? But that has been the problem; a rational view of the world has no consideration for an emotional intuitive view or any other view of the world, so unfortunately, we have all been looking through the wrong end of a telescope. Consequently, rationality only sees the world from a very narrow distorted viewpoint which leads to a reversal of reality, a mirror image of a true humanitarian reality. Rationalism, logic and reason are all dismissive of our irrational emotions and feelings, but they have 'thrown the baby out with the bathwater *and* the bath', with them went the reality of humanity's aspirations hopes and dreams, absolute eternal values and principles, love, wisdom, compassion, empathy, understanding, immortality, and the ability to experience the only reality that eventually counts, the reality of God. But out also went the ability to understand the spirit of the law; the ego only knows the letter of the law and because of that is corruptible, prone to the seduction of immediate commercial gain, short term fixes with no long term planning for the future of humanity, and condemned to disagree on absolutely everything. We all have to consider the distinct probability that rationalism, whose agent is the ego, is the collective delusion from which we all suffer, a mental straightjacket that will not allow us to see any other possibilities. The ego's thinking, its mind, the brain's intelligence, rationalism, logic, reason and all those people who place such great faith in them are going to be shocked to find that emotional wisdom and understanding are ultimately far superior to all of them combined, and stunned to realise they are not actually the person they think they are, still something of an imposter and a pale reflection of their real selves.

I cannot help but arrive at the natural and inevitable conclusion from the evidence, that the ego is not just stupid, it is completely insane, e.g. it is deluded, suffers from megalomania, ideas of grandeur, e.g. "there is no other god but me", it is paranoid, it reverses then denies reality, it suffers from visual and auditory hallucinations in that it sees and hears what it wants to, then does not see or hear things that are *actually* there, e.g. the evidence, injustice, suffering and its own behaviour, all of which can be summed up in the final symptom, denial. Most of these are first rank symptoms of mental illness in the ICD 10, the official diagnostic tool used in psychiatry, and which could define this illness as schizophrenia, not a split personality, but a split with reality. This raises the interesting spectre whereby everyone deemed to be sane are actually insane according to the official definition of mental illness, and all those diagnosed as mentally ill are actually those ones amongst us trying to make sense of an insane world, albeit in vain. R. D. Laing stated that "Insanity is a sane response to an insane world", but equally sanity is an *insane* response to an insane world. Laing did not have a theory on to which to nail his observations, but now there is one, 'The theory of the schizophrenic ego'. It all sounds ludicrous I know, but it is probably the truth because logically, this is the only way that the world, as it exists, and our complete indifference to the injustice and suffering, makes any sense at all. We have all become insulated from and inured to the plight of the weak, the poor and oppressed in society; *we* have become split from their reality, and this is just in Britain. The mechanisms that the ego uses to create this split from reality are projection and denial, it is like a magicians illusion, all done with mirrors, which makes an insane world appear sane. The ego protects us from reality, but in doing so divorces us from that reality. Psychiatry unwittingly connives with society in maintaining the agreed reality, we are all united in social collusion together. This is the cosmetic procedure society uses to maintain the status quo, it is mass insanity, but this illusion will only stretch so far and shows signs of coming apart. The concept of mental illness is the big stick which society wields in order to ensure we all comply with the agreed insanity and remain locked into this collective delusion of a looking glass world; a compliant frightened mass group conformity that dares not see any other reality; we dare not see, or be allowed to see, that the world we have created is insane.

The mentally ill are society's scapegoats, they serve that social function so that society does not have to change, so it does not have to address the problem of an insane world; and the irony is, it is those who are more sensitive, and react to living in an insane world, who become the ones labelled insane, the ones who are supposedly split from reality, when in fact they are the ones who are more in touch with reality and it is that reality which has made them unwell. The mentally ill are split from society's definition of reality, but it is that reality that is in question. The ego is only doing what it thinks it has to do to help you to survive in an insane world, but that strategy is to deny reality, project on to others, to blame others, to reverse reality, to block off our emotions and feelings, reject humanities aspirations, turn a blind eye to the real causes of suffering in the world and in the process deny the reality of God. The mentally ill are the ones diagnosed insane, but it is we who are actually the ones who are separated from reality, the reality of an unjust world; we are all locked into this insane reality within our individual ego's capsule of safety, because this is the agreed consensus of our opinion leaders who cannot see any other way of being: we are all schizophrenic now.

Mental illness is an opportunity for the individual to find their true selves and become a whole person again, but psychiatry won't let that happen, it is extremely rational, it does not countenance this nonsense for one moment, its remit is to ensure we all comply with the agreed consensus of opinion, because if you don't then you must be mentally ill, but 'there is a turd in the punchbowl'. Psychiatry's objective is to heal the ego and not destroy it, but in doing so it limits the opportunity for that individual to become truly sane. The ones labelled mentally ill are the ones most sensitive to the world in which we live, they are the litmus test for a sane world, perhaps we should listen to them. The concern is that the people with the biggest egos are the ones who rise to the top of the pile. The people who run the country, our politicians, bankers, company directors, the media barons, the people who take the decisions that affect our lives, the opinion leaders, the very people who keep us locked into this insane world are not only the most foolish amongst us but are also the most insane, the most divorced from reality; and these people have their finger on *our* nuclear button.

This is a plea to the human race; pause for one moment from the chaos of your everyday life, step out of that self-imposed tomb, throw off the chains that bind you and blind you, take a look around, see through God's eyes and through humanities eyes, and see the world as it really is, and from that vantage point it will be clear to you that the world we have created is a looking glass world in which everything is the wrong way round in human terms, it is insane, it is the exact opposite of the world your heart would have chosen if given the choice. In a world where profit is king, humanity becomes a beggar on the street. What sort of a world do you want to leave to your children and your grandchildren? The choice is still ours; just. The human race is stuck in a primitive chaotic world, hell-bent on an accelerating roller-coaster ride to oblivion and cannot get off, that dares not get off, nobody dare admit that maybe something is seriously wrong with this world we have created, after all, we can't all be wrong can we; can we? We can't stop the world and get off, so we have to stop selfishly squabbling and competing over the petty pieces, who's got the most, the biggest or the best; these are all trivial distractions from the real meaning of life and in the end we all lose. There is a much greater treasure available to all of us which, ironically, the ego is blind to because of its selfish greed: surely God does exist. We have to pull together for the common good so we all win; rise above the letter of the law, and start building the bigger picture.

"It's so obviously just too preposterous for words that everything we have ever believed to be true about ourselves and human nature throughout history is in fact false", but that is the enormity of what I am asking you to accept. We need more than just rationalism to forge our future because it will surely take us into the abyss, we need greater wisdom and a New Enlightenment. This is not a theory anymore, it is a truth whose time has now come. You may now see the enormous implications of the secret contained in Poussin and Teniers' paintings, it turns everything on its head. The ego should have been looking through the other end of the telescope where it would have seen a much bigger picture, a landscape where elephants roam freely.

The rational, highly intelligent ego thinks it is so clever, but like the ship without a keel it lacks direction, no purpose in life, no meaning in life except to accrue more and more possessions, which in the end becomes meaningless. Through our emotions and feelings, our spirit and soul know intuitively the direction in life they have to travel, they are the keel and rudder that understand the spirit of the law. There is no time to endlessly debate the virtues or not of this new knowledge, that would be like fiddling whilst Rome burns or discussing the likelihood of getting wet now that your *Titanic* is sinking: you are about to be plunged into reality. Time is running out, this is no time to philosophise, it's time to fill the lifeboats or start swimming like mad, using your *arms* of course. How apt that Freud's analogy for the unconscious, the iceberg, should be the metaphor for what finally sinks the unsinkable, *HMS Capitalism*, let's see how Captain Ego gets out of this one, it's sink or swim time, "remember to use those arms, we should make Arcadia 'by midday'." Let's hope we make it, the sooner the better, the alternative, doing nothing means we all 'go down together', the year is 2013 and the clock is ticking. Social observers should take note of the ego, capitalism, society and the media's response to this challenge; now that the issue has been raised, doing nothing is not an option, you don't want to become a 'denier', do you? Humanity has to strive for that New Jerusalem if only for our children's sake, the alternative is hell here on Earth.

There is a great treasure available to everyone of all nations and creeds, which is our natural inheritance bequeathed to us by God.

It was lost to humanity by a careless World Church and its blind leaders and which has left a hole, a great void at the centre of our spirituality. A little sparrow stumbled upon this treasure accidentally one day whilst scratting around for food in the wilderness. A glint caught the eye, from something hanging in a bush, something which had been discarded, rejected, unwanted, disowned, like something cast out. Even though tarnished from all the years of neglect, it was still the most beautiful necklace sparrow had ever seen. Once cleaned and polished it was hung back where it rightfully belonged, without want of reward, at the heart of all world religions, so that others can share in its beauty and so that it would always be accessible again to humankind.

This is the truth based on the Gnostic philosophy revealed by the secret contained in Poussin and Teniers' paintings. I think you can guess where I stand on this, I don't just believe it's the truth: I know. It is up to you whether you accept it or not, it is open to debate, but you will need a good reason and a strong argument against to reject it. You can either bury your head in the sand and ignore it, throw scorn on it, deny it by pretending you never read this book; or you could stop laughing at frogs, stop listening to your ego and begin the greatest journey of your life, the greatest adventure there is, the voyage of self-discovery. I cannot take you any further, nobody can do this one for you, you have to do it for yourself; you are on your own now, follow your heart, seek God and you will find. Strive to be ordinary and when you have achieved that, then you will have become extraordinary. Be your humble and honest self; empty your heart of all arrogant and selfish pretensions, and God will find you. The challenge is there for everyone, you have to try it before you can reject it. If you find you are vehemently opposed to the ideas put forward here, then ask yourself why, what is it that objects? Why are you afraid of losing control? Why are you afraid of your emotions and feelings? Why are you afraid of love? Why are you afraid of life? Why are you afraid of losing your rationality? Why are you afraid of losing nothing and gaining all?

You are one of the fortunate few who have been given this one chance to achieve immortality, don't miss out now because of your own doubts and fears, you cannot plead ignorance now, you have to be brave enough and have enormous faith in the eventual outcome to risk everything. There is no time to lose, life *is* a rehearsal you know, we have to get it right in this life to reach the next. "Bon voyage."

This is no hoax, these are just the signs of the times. This is an idea whose time has come, this is the future, a new spiritual age, a spiritual renaissance, a New Age of Enlightenment. This is the dawning of the age of Aquarius and these are the chimes of freedom, this is your wake up call, a shake to the world, a kiss from a prince for Sleeping Beauty, a kiss for a frog from a princess, the sound of a sword being drawn from a stone, the sound of one small child crying in the wilderness. This was 2012, the end of the Mayan calendar, not the end of the world, but a new beginning, a new era. This is the Apocalypse in the true sense of the meaning of the Greek word, 'as in the lifting of a veil', the real Armageddon, the fight between good and evil takes place within you. The little urchin, the fool, a simple soul, the beggar on the street, a stray cat, the lamb of God, sparrow, the scapegoat that did not know it was supposed to die in the wilderness and has now returned to confront the ego and capitalism not only with their own sins and crimes against humanity, but also with the irrationality of their rationalism and the insanity of the world they have created. This child of God, rejected, abandoned, disowned by each and every one of you, untouchable, pariah of the world, orphan of humanity. The future starts here at this moment in time, today is the first day of the rest of your spiritual and immortal life, this is the Truth, this is the Way, this is the Love, this is the Light; this is our Destiny. Funny how we never saw it coming, but swiftly, silently, suddenly and without warning, 'The Year of the Lord' is probably upon us.

Epilogue

The teacher asked the class, "Which bird can fly the highest?" After considerable thought the children came up with a unanimous decision, "The eagle." But the answer that the teacher gave surprised them. It was "the smallest bird of all," because it does not matter how high the eagle flies, the little bird can always ride on its back and at the very last moment fly just that little bit higher

Acknowledgements

I would like to thank Bill Kersey at DEK publications for permission to use images of Manuscript II from his book *The Accursed Treasure of Rennes-le-Chateau* which I have referred to as parchment three in this book. The Louvre Museum, Paris, for images of *The Shepherds of Arcadia II* by Nicolas Poussin. The author has made every effort to trace and contact all copyright holders of reproduced copyright material in this book. I have been unable to trace the copyright owner of the painting *St Anthony and St Paul in the desert* by David Teniers the Younger, the last known whereabouts being when it was bought anonymously in 1927 by someone in Spain, or so the story goes. Previous authors on the subject have acknowledged the Western Art Library at the Ashmolean Museum as their source, but on contacting them, they insist they have never had this painting or print in their collection. I have been unable to use this image because there appears to be nobody to obtain permission from. Sometimes the copyright law is an ass.

Many thanks to E. Djacenta without whom this book could never have been written and who was a constant source of valuable advice, encouragement, wisdom and knowledge.

Mam, Dad, Bryan and Marilyn who created a happy secure and loving family life; we felt so wealthy, we didn't know we were actually poor. Jennie who set the fool on his way. Corinne who rescued a tramp slumped in a doorway, quenched his thirst, stood him up, dusted him down, and set him on his way. Pam who provided a simple soul with the final piece to a jigsaw puzzle; problem was, it took him over twenty years to remember what he'd done with the rest of the pieces.

Anita, my partner for over twenty years and long suffering wife, especially whilst I have been writing this book, who took in a stray cat and gave it shelter. We have two grown up boys now, Jed and Matt, and the most amazing thing is, she has not set me on my way yet, I think she must have forgotten I still live here, and family life has returned to being happy and normal once more, well, most of the time, which was all I ever wanted.

APPENDIX 1

The Nicene Creed

(more properly called the Nicene-Constantinople Creed) which is a revision of the Creed of Nicaea (325) from the great Council of Constantinople in AD 381.

We believe in one God, the Father, the Almighty, maker of heaven and earth, of all that is seen and unseen. We believe in one Lord, Jesus Christ, the only Son of God, eternally begotten of the Father, God from God, Light from Light, true God from true God, begotten, not made, of one being with the Father. Through him all things were made. For us and for our salvation he came down from heaven. By the power of the Holy Spirit he became incarnate from the Virgin Mary, and was made man. For our sake he was crucified under Pontius Pilate, he suffered death and was buried. On the third day he rose again in accordance with the Scriptures. He ascended in heaven and is seated at the right hand of the Father. He will come again in glory to judge the living and the dead, and his kingdom will have no end. We believe in the Holy Spirit, the Lord, the giver of life, who proceeds from the Father (and the son). With the Father and the Son he is worshipped and glorified. He has spoken through the Prophets. We believe in one holy Catholic and Apostolic Church. We acknowledge one baptism for the forgiveness of sins. We look for the resurrection of the dead, and the life of the world to come.
Amen.

REFERENCES

Andrews, Richard and Schellenberger, Paul (1996) 'The Tomb of God', Time Warner Books

Baigent, Michael Leigh, Richard and Lincoln, Henry (1982) 'The Holy Blood and The Holy Grail', Jonathan Cape

Corjan de Raaf and Jean-Pierre d'Aniort (undated) 'Written in stone, the secret of Coumesourde', Andrew Gough's Arcadia

Damasio, Antonio R. (2005) 'The science of emotions', Scientific American March 24

De Sède, Gérard (2001) 'The Accursed Treasure of Rennes-le-Chateau', Translated from the Original French by Bill Kersey, DEK

Dychtwald, Kenneth (1977) 'Bodymind', Pantheon Books

Freke, Timothy and Gandy, Peter (1999) 'The Pagan Mysteries behind early Christianity', from 'The Jesus Mysteries: was the original Jesus a Pagan God?' in, 'Secrets of the Code' by Dan Burstein (2004), W & N

Illich, Ivan D. (1971) 'Deschooling Society', Pelican

Lepinois (1656), 'Lettres de Louis Fouquet' p 269

Lincoln, Henry (1991) 'The Holy Place', Arris

Pagels, Elaine (1980) 'One God, One Bishop', from 'The Gnostic Gospels', Pelican

The Nag Hammadi Library 'The Hypostasis of the Archons', 89.11-91.1 pp 154-5

The Nag Hammadi Library 'The Gospel of Thomas' 32.10-11 p 118 and 45.29-33 p 126

Norvill, Roy (1986) 'Hermes Unveiled' Ashgrove

Poe, Edgar Allan (1845) 'The Gold Bug' in Poe's Tales Wiley and

Putnam

Reich, Wilhelm (1972) 'Character Analysis' Touchstone

Rousseau, Jean Jacques (1762) 'The Social Contract', Wikipedia

Robinson, Tony (2005) 'The Real Da Vinci Code', Channel 4 TV

De Sede, Gerrard (1967) 'L'Or de Rennes' Published in paperback
   as 'Le Trésor Maudit' Juillard, Paris

Szasz, Thomas (1960) 'The Myth of Mental Illness' in Amer.
   Psychol.15 113-8, 68-9

BIBLIOGRAPHY

Allegro, John (1987) 'The Dead Sea Scrolls', Pelican

Avalon, Arthur (1974) 'The Serpent Power', Dover

Baker, Elsworth (1974) 'Man in the Trap', Avon, New York

Blavatsky, Madame H.P. (1877) 'Isis Unveiled', vol. 1 and 2, Theosophical Publishing House

Brunton, Paul (1970) 'Quest of the Overself', Rider, London

Brunton, Paul (1969) 'The Hidden Teaching Behind Yoga', Rider, London

Burckhardt, Titus (1986) 'Alchemy', Element

Conway, David (1987) 'Secret Wisdom', Aquarian

Dee, John (1985) 'The Rosie Crucian Secrets', Aquarian

Eliade, Mircea (1973) 'Yoga: Immortality and Freedom', Princeton Bolingen

Evola, Julius (1995) 'The Hermetic Tradition', Inner Traditions International

Jung, C.G. (1953) 'Psychology and Alchemy', Routledge

Jung, C.G. (1983) 'Alchemical Studies', RKP

King, Francis (1986) 'Tantra for Westerners', Aquarian

Lapidus (1976) 'In Pursuit of Gold', Neville Spearman, Suffolk

Luk, Charles (1984) 'Taoist Yoga: Alchemy and Immortality', Weiser

Mookerjee, Ajit (1982) 'Kundalini', Thames and Hudson

The Nag Hammadi Library (1977) Leiden

Putnam B. and Wood J. E. (2003) 'The Treasure of Rennes le Chateau', Sutton

Rama, Swami, Ballentine, Rudolf and Ajaya, Swami (1976) 'Yoga and Psychotherapy', Himalayan Institute

Stanford, Peter (1997) 'The Devil: A Biography' Mandarin

The Hermetic Museum (1997) Taschen
Van Lisebeth, Andre (1979) 'Pranayama', Allen and Unwin
Wilhelm, Richard (1987) 'The Secret of the Golden Flower', Arkana
Wood, David (1985) 'Genisis', The Baton Press

Lightning Source UK Ltd.
Milton Keynes UK
UKOW03f0043181213

223230UK00002B/28/P